1 0 0

FAVORITE

ROSES

1 0 0
F AVORITE
R OSES

TERI DUNN

MetroBooks

DEDICATION

Thanks to my Jackson & Perkins friends: Estin Kiger, Larry Levinger,

Barbara Mount, Ginny Egan, Kathy Pyle, Stevie Lindh, Joyce Tonkin,

Caron Yakubec, Mike Cady, and the Queen of Roses, Lorie Harmon.

And for Shawn, Wes, and Tris, with all my love.

MetroBooks

An Imprint of Friedman/Fairfax Publishers

© 1998 by Michael Friedman Publishing Group, Inc.

Library of Congress Cataloging-in-Publication

Dunn, Teri.
         100 favorite roses   / by Teri Dunn.
                 p.   cm.
            ISBN 1-56799-435-0
      1. Roses.   2. Rose culture.   I. Title.
      SB411.D78   1997
      635.9'33372-- dc20
                                              96-34521
                                                  CIP

Editors: Susan Lauzau and Rachel Simon
Art Director: Lynne Yeamans
Designer: Millie Sensat
Photography Editor: Wendy Missan

Color separations by Ocean Graphic Co. Ltd.
Printed in Singapore by KHL Printing Co. Ltd.

For bulk purchases and special sales, please contact:
Friedman/Fairfax Publishers
Attention: Sales Department
15 West 26th Street
New York, NY 10010
212/685-6610 FAX 212/685-1307

Visit our website: http://www.metrobooks.com

Photography credits:

©David Coppin: 12, 14, 23, 31, 36, 38, 47, 70, 71, 79, 89,
   96, 105

©R. Todd Davis: 22, 49, 53, 91, 102

©Alan Detrick: 28

©Alan & Linda Detrick: 21, 40, 56, 57, 99

©Derek Fell: 6, 19, 66, 74, 75, 78, 84, 87, 108, 109

Courtesy Flower Carpet: 46

©John Glover: 30

Courtesy Jackson & Perkins: 64, 68, 72, 81

©Dency Kane: 13, 15, 20, 24, 25, 27, 29, 32, 33, 34, 43, 44,
45, 50, 52, 55, 58, 60, 65, 69, 83, 85, 92, 95, 98, 101, 104, 107,
112, 114, 115

©Mike Lowe: 100, 110

©Charles Mann: 2, 9, 16, 37, 88, 97, 117

©Clive Nichols: 17, 54

Courtesy Nor'East Miniature Roses, Inc.: 86

©Jerry Pavia: 51, 76

Photo/Nats, Inc.: ©Priscilla Connell: 94; ©Wally Eberhart:
41, 90; Robert E. Lyons: 67, 82; ©Ann Reilly: 35, 39, 48,
61, 62, 63, 73, 93, 106; ©John J. Smith: 77; ©Albert
Squillace: 59, 103, 111; ©Kim Todd: 18; ©Virginia
Twinam-Smith: 10, 116

©Nance S. Truworthy: 26

©Suzanne Verrier: 11, 42, 80, 113

CONTENTS

Introduction   6

     HOW TO SELECT A ROSE PLANT

     HOW TO PLANT A ROSE

     BASIC ROSE CARE

     ROSE TROUBLESHOOTING

100 Favorite Roses A−Z   10

Plant Hardiness Zones   118

Sources   119

Introduction

Everybody knows roses are among the most splendid, most beloved flowers in the world. But not everybody grows them, perhaps because there are some unfortunate misconceptions about them. Traditional rows of hybrid tea roses emerging from a bed of bare earth or bark chips may strike present-day gardeners as boring or stilted. But roses, from hybrid teas to climbers to the newer groundcovering varieties, don't have to be confined to bedding schemes. They can contribute wonderful exuberance to today's popular "mixed" or "naturalistic" gardens of perennials and shrubs. And they often have the bonus of providing more constant color than their companions throughout the course of a summer.

It's also a myth that roses are high-maintenance, requiring all sorts of special pruning and continual spraying just to remain presentable. Rose breeders have been hard at work dispelling these problems. And dedicated rosarians keep tabs on roses past, present, and future, winnowing out the very best. These factors should certainly ease a beginner's worries. A well-chosen rose requires no more special maintenance than many other garden plants. The truth is, there's a great deal of variety in the rose world, and any gardener, no matter where he or she lives, can grow at least one showpiece rose easily and well.

The roses in this book were selected based on two sets of criteria. First, they exhibit some of the finest qualities a gardener could wish for: dependable growth, longevity, winter-hardiness, beautiful blooms, and, in many cases, heady fragrance. Second, they are readily available (check your local garden center or order from the mail-order catalogs listed on page 119). Some are old favorites that have stood the test of time, others are terrific new hybrids—the goal was to include a cross section.

Not all of these will grow well everywhere, so read the individual descriptions to see if the rose of your dreams will be happy in your garden. You may also wish to double-check with your local consulting rosarian. The American Rose Society has an entire network of these experts; call or write the society for the one nearest you (see the appendix for the address and phone number).

How to Select a Rose Plant

There are many different kinds of roses, from low-growing groundcovers to classic bushes and hedge types to lusty, towering climbers. Some produce flowers in clusters (these are called floribundas) and others are primarily one-to-a-stem (hybrid teas). Some bloom with abandon just once in the spring or early summer, and others repeat on and off throughout the summer.

No matter where you buy a rose plant, you will find yourself confronted with two choices: potted or bareroot. It's easy to be seduced by the container-grown roses that look already established in potting mix, leafed out and maybe even showing colored buds. But these plants are not the best choice. Rose roots require plenty of room, and too often pot-grown roses are crammed in or potbound, which damages them and inhibits future good growth. Also, the potting mix is quite different (lighter, less dense, and often less fertile) than your garden's soil. The container-grown rose plant is likely to have trouble "leaving home," that is, spreading out beyond its original boundaries as it must to grow and thrive.

If you shop for your rose at a garden center in the spring, choose what looks like the best plant. Look for strong, healthy canes and roots—avoid those that show signs of damage or dehydration. If you're buying a pot-grown plant, at least insist on one in a relatively large container in the hope that the roots are still in good shape. It'll experience less transplant trauma and you'll have more to look forward to if it's just beginning to show signs of life rather than fully leafed out or blooming.

Bareroot plants are sometimes available at garden centers and are the form of choice for mail-order houses. They may look like dry sticks, but don't be deceived by appearances—these are always your best buy. Bareroot plants are dormant, which means that they can be planted earlier than potted roses. They will adapt to the soil in your garden gradually and without transplant trauma, easing into growth at a natural pace.

At garden centers, you'll sometimes find bareroot plants tucked into cardboard or plastic sleeves, protected by a moisture-retaining medium like wood shavings. If possible, slide out your choice and examine it carefully. Don't buy one with dried-out or blackened, wiry roots. The canes should also be in good shape and not yet leafing out.

Mail-order specialists offer a tantalizing array of roses, including many wonderful varieties you'll never find locally. You'll also get the expert information and landscaping ideas, customer service, and a guarantee that a garden center rarely offers.

How to Plant a Rose

If you plant a rose correctly—not a mysterious or difficult process—the plant is sure to do well for you. First of all, though, pick a good site, one in full sun with decent, well-drained soil and a little shelter from drying winds.

Prepare a good hole. Make it about 2 feet (60cm) wide, and, for the bareroot plant, about 18 inches (45cm) deep. A potted rose's hole should be just a little deeper than the depth of the container you bought it in. Then, loosen the bottom and sides of the hole to make it easier for the roots to penetrate the surrounding soil.

BAREROOT ROSES

Soak the plant in a bucket of water for a few hours or overnight before planting to rehydrate it. If you wish, add a small amount of liquid fertilizer to stimulate root growth, plus a tablespoon or two of household bleach to prevent the growth of unwanted bacteria.

When you're ready to plant, take some of the soil you removed while digging the hole and make a mound or cone all the way up. Pack it in place firmly with your hands. You'll find that the bareroot plant's root system's naturally splayed-out form rests easily on the mound. While holding the stem in place with one hand, check that the roots are not tangled and are facing downward. The "bud union" area—the knob where the rose stem meets the root system—should be at ground level (a little lower if you have cold winters, that is, Zones 6 and north). If it's not at ground level, simply add or take away soil on the mound until it's right.

You will refill the hole in two steps. Mix some organic matter, such as compost or aged cow manure, into the soil you've removed and scoop this mix into the hole until it's about halfway full. Sprinkle in some slow-release rose fertil-

izer, bonemeal, and/or superphosphate to nourish the roots. Then add water until the hole is filled to the top. After it drains, finish backfilling. Finally, lay an inch or two (2.5 or 5cm) of mulch such as compost or bark chips to suppress weeds and retain soil moisture.

POTTED ROSES

Gently ease the plant out of the pot and score the sides of the root ball with the side of your trowel or a knife—this loosens it up and allows new roots to form. Place the plant in the hole, and fill in around it with soil amended as described above for the bareroot rose. Firm it into place with your hands, and water well to make sure there are no air pockets. Then mulch around the base of the plant.

BASIC ROSE CARE

WATER

Roses should be watered at least once or twice a week during the summer, and more often only if the plants are obviously wilting. They prefer deep soakings. Always water at ground level, as damp foliage is more susceptible to disease.

FERTILIZER

Roses love food, rewarding the gardener with vigorous growth and fabulous blooms. What to feed roses is a matter of debate. There are products labeled "just for roses" as well as general-use, balanced fertilizers that serve perfectly well. Epsom salts (magnesium sulfate) are often recommended as a supplement because they stimulate "basal growth," that is, new, major canes. Whatever you use, distribute it generously around the rose's "drip line" (the imaginary line along the bush's outer perimeter) and water it in well.

PRUNING

Wait until early spring, after danger of hard frost is past so new growth doesn't get nipped. Begin by cutting out all "nonnegotiable" growth, such as canes that are winter-damaged, diseased, unshapely, or rubbing against others. Then remove all thin growth, anything smaller in diameter than a pencil. Finally, remove all but five to ten strong canes. Prune the canes that are left, cutting back up to, but no more than, half of a cane's length. That's all there is to it. Your rose will be reinvigorated and soon burst into robust growth. Note: there are some roses that do not require such drastic pruning every single spring. Over the years, keep an eye on yours and the way it's growing and decide if you wish to be more conservative.

ROSE TROUBLESHOOTING

While it's true that roses can fall prey to pests and diseases, it's not true that a rose gardener has to spend the summer doing constant battle. Begin by choosing a rose that is known to grow well in your area. And remember that a rose that starts out healthy is much more likely to remain that way; so plant it well and care for it as described above. Other tips: be sure each rose has plenty of air circulation.

And keep the area around the plant tidy: rake up fallen leaves and clip out growth that looks unhealthy. Prevention is always easier than crisis intervention!

Should your rose show signs of trouble, diagnose and treat it early rather than letting the problem continue. When you must spray, use a product specifically labeled for the problem, follow label directions to the letter, and treat the plant on a dry, windless day.

'Abraham Darby'

TYPE/CLASS: English shrub

HEIGHT: 5 feet (1.5m); 10 feet (3m) as a climber

BLOOM SIZE: 4½ to 5 inches (10cm)

BLOOM TIME: repeats all summer

FRAGRANCE: strong

'Abraham Darby'

This lush-flowered rose is romance itself. The color is downright glorious, a warm apricot with yellow undertones that make the blossom seem lit from within. And the fragrance is delicious—rich and generous, especially in hot sun. The plant makes a big, splendid bush, and because it has lanky, arching stems, you can also train it as a climber. Just watch out for the thorns, which are stout and sharp, up to an inch (2.5cm) long! Fortunately, it doesn't require much pruning and maintains a naturally tidy shape.

'Abraham Darby' is the work of famous English rose breeder David Austin, and like all of his roses, it combines the best qualities of the old-fashioned varieties (sumptuous yet soft color, powerful fragrance, loads of petals for a very full blossom) with the best of the newer hybrids (constant bloom, disease-resistance). Indeed, 'Abraham Darby' may be one of the most disease-resistant English roses around.

'*Agnes*'

TYPE/CLASS: rugosa hybrid

HEIGHT: 4–7 feet (1.2–2.4m)

BLOOM SIZE: 3½ inches (8cm)

BLOOM TIME: early summer

FRAGRANCE: strong

'Agnes'

Here's your opportunity to grow a very tough rose with delicately beautiful blooms. 'Agnes' is an older cultivar that has stood the test of time, particularly in cold northern gardens. She was also the first yellow-flowered rugosa, and is still considered by many to be the best.

The blooms are a wonderful shade of pastel yellow (the intensity of the color varies, depending on the weather), fluffy with petals, and have a heady, fruity fragrance. Like all rugosas, this plant has dark green, crinkly leaves, plenty of thorns, and is extremely disease-resistant. If the rest of your garden follows a soft-colored theme, try 'Agnes' as an ideal "garden room" boundary or property-line hedge.

'Altissimo'

TYPE/CLASS: climber

HEIGHT: 8–12 feet (2.4–3.7m)

BLOOM SIZE: 5–6 inches (13–15cm)

BLOOM TIME: repeats all summer

FRAGRANCE: medium

'Altissimo'

Somewhat unusual among climbers, this lusty bloomer has single flowers, which simply means they have few petals (five to seven per flower). They're a brilliant shade of crimson, centered by golden stamens, and when they open fully, the flower is breathtaking. They also have a sweet — but not overpowering — rose-perfume fragrance. The dark green foliage is large, robust, and especially disease-resistant.

Another nice thing about 'Altissimo' is that it blooms along its full length, not just toward its top. Be sure to showcase this one; don't relegate it to the back fence. 'Altissimo' would be terrific clambering up a pergola or wide archway, or even just trained up a pillar. It can also be espaliered against a wall.

'America'

TYPE/CLASS: climber

HEIGHT: 9–12 feet (2.7–3.7m)

BLOOM SIZE: 3½–4½ inches (8–11cm)

BLOOM TIME: repeats all summer

FRAGRANCE: medium

'America'

The American Rose Society has given out plenty of awards over the years, but rarely to climbers, so it's significant that 'America' was so honored in 1976. It's a classy rose, with handsomely formed blossoms of coral-pink. Loaded with petals, these blossoms retain the classic hybrid-tea shape and are quite symmetrical. They're also fragrant, with a rich, orange blossom scent. Plus, they appear in clusters, creating a feeling of graceful abundance. The plant itself is a vigorous grower, bushy with medium green leaves, and disease-resistant. (If mildew is a concern in your area, make sure the plant gets good air circulation.)

'America' can be used any number of ways; plant it as a tall upright shrub or train it as an archway showpiece. The form and color are both versatile enough to lend charm to a cottage garden or dignity to a more formal setting.

'American Pillar'

TYPE/CLASS: climber/rambler

HEIGHT: 12–20 feet (3.7–6m) or more

BLOOM SIZE: 2–3 inches (5–7.5cm)

BLOOM TIME: late spring–early summer

FRAGRANCE: none

'American Pillar'

This classic rose from the turn of the century has a casual, summer-vacation feel to it, perhaps because we've seen it adorning old summer cottages or cascading over a venerable tree in someone's "back forty." It flowers in extravagant sprays, with literally dozens of blooms per cluster. Each one sports only five hot pink petals, with a crisp white center and a sunburst of yellow stamens. The plant pumps out blooms for weeks, often up to a full month running. A performance this exuberant makes you forgive the lack of fragrance!

The plant itself is easygoing, with glossy green leaves and long, somewhat thorny, pliable canes that lend themselves well to training if you keep after it. Indeed, it will submit willingly to life on an arbor or arch. But left to its own devices, 'American Pillar' is a rambler at heart.

'Angel Face'

TYPE/CLASS: floribunda

HEIGHT: 2–3 feet (60–90cm)

BLOOM SIZE: 3½–4 inches (8–10cm)

BLOOM TIME: repeats all summer

FRAGRANCE: strong

'Angel Face'

You get a lot of fabulous, rich fragrance from this low-growing, mounding rose. Like all floribundas, it blooms mainly in clusters rather than one-to-a-stem, displaying the flowers in all stages of development, from full, pointed buds to completely open. The open flowers are truly gorgeous: a rich, deep mauve, touched with red. They're thick with ruffle-edged petals, so the effect is as lush and feminine as a Victorian greeting card.

The bush is healthy, with lots of dark foliage that has a slight coppery tint to it, a nice complement to the flowers. It is also of a manageable size, making it well-suited to smaller gardens or bedding schemes. You could even tuck one into a perennial border for color and fragrance throughout the summer. For all its superb qualities, 'Angel Face' won an All-America Rose Selections award in 1969.

'Ballerina'

TYPE/CLASS: hybrid musk/polyantha

HEIGHT: 3–6 feet (1–1.8m)

BLOOM SIZE: 1–2 inches (2.5–5cm)

BLOOM TIME: repeats all summer

FRAGRANCE: slight

'Ballerina'

No doubt this lovely rose got its name from its graceful arching stems. Yet the plant has discipline—it is dense with smallish, dark leaves and stays compact, growing about as wide as it does tall. This makes it ideal for a specimen plant, placed out in the open where nobody can fail to admire its charms. But it will also work well as a natural-looking hedge or draped over a low fence.

The dainty, single-form flowers are on the small side, but produced in generous numbers on luxurious tresses of up to a hundred individual blooms. The petals are a fancy pink that darkens toward the outer edges and are centered with a creamy white eye and dark yellow stamens. Like others of its kind, 'Ballerina' has a musky, but subtle, perfume.

'Barbara Bush'

TYPE/CLASS: hybrid tea

HEIGHT: 5 feet (1.5m)

BLOOM SIZE: 5 inches (13cm)

BLOOM TIME: repeats all summer

FRAGRANCE: slight

'Barbara Bush'

There are many pink roses in the world, but this one, named for the former U.S. First Lady, has a robust character and splendid, high-quality blooms. While other pinks flag in the heat of summer, 'Barbara Bush' continues to produce a steady parade of beautiful blossoms. Not a pure pink, they are softer, almost porcelainlike, toward the center, and have a darker, watercolor-brushed pink to the outer petal edges.

As with most hybrid teas, the flowers are produced on single stems, and you'll certainly be tempted to harvest them for bouquets.

The plant itself is strong-growing and disease-resistant, with glossy, dark green leaves that set a handsome stage for the blooms. Its shape is upright and vaselike, making it a regal addition to any garden.

'Beauty Secret'

TYPE/CLASS: miniature

HEIGHT: 10–18 inches (25–45cm)

BLOOM SIZE: 1½ inches (4cm)

BLOOM TIME: repeats all summer

FRAGRANCE: strong

'Beauty Secret'

The American Rose Society bestowed an Award of Excellence upon this precious little plant in 1975. All season long it is laden with terrific, double, dark red blooms that have the formal perfection of larger hybrid tea blooms. Even the buds are fancy, looking just like tiny replicas of those on the long-stemmed red roses of Valentine's Day. All this, plus they're sweetly fragrant.

Like the best minis, the plant is clothed in glossy, dark leaves, and grows vigorously to its full height. 'Beauty Secret' makes a wonderful container-grown rose, particularly if you have an especially pretty pot in mind, something fancier than mere terra-cotta. It can also be grown directly in the ground, but will require winter protection.

'Betty Prior'

TYPE/CLASS: floribunda

HEIGHT: 5–7 feet (1.5–2m)

BLOOM SIZE: 3–3½ inches (7.5–8cm)

BLOOM TIME: repeats all summer

FRAGRANCE: medium

'Betty Prior'

For gardeners who live in the cold North (Zones 5 on up), this rose is a godsend. Not only is it especially hardy, it is a generous bloomer. The flowers are often likened to those of a pink-flowering dogwood tree. Sporting only five slightly ruffled petals and centered with a small boss of yellow stamens, they open to a saucer shape and hold that form well for days. Borne in bountiful clusters, they literally cover the plant with color. Their delicious (though not overpowering) scent can be detected from several feet away.

Many rosarians have remarked that 'Betty Prior' has a nice "wild rose" look—but it is better-behaved. Given that quality, and the fact that it is tall for a floribunda, and rather full, the best use for this agreeable rose may be as a hedge or in a row along a fence.

'Blanc Double de Coubert'

TYPE/CLASS: rugosa hybrid

HEIGHT: 5–7 feet (1.5–2m)

BLOOM SIZE: 2½–3 inches (6.5–7.5cm)

BLOOM TIME: repeats all summer

FRAGRANCE: strong

'Blanc Double de Coubert'

The crisp combination of pure white blooms and dark green leaves makes this shrubby rose a knockout. The flowers are flush with a double load of petals, giving them an almost camellialike appearance, and they have an intense clove fragrance. The peak show is in early summer, but you'll have encores throughout the summer. Nor is that the end: autumn brings another remarkable color duet, this time showcasing big, orange-red hips against a backdrop of bright yellow foliage.

'Blanc Double de Coubert' is a rugosa type, which means that it is exceptionally tough, tolerating poor soil, cold winters (to Zone 3), wind, and salt, and shrugging off pests and diseases. The trade-off comes in the somewhat coarsely textured foliage, the thorny canes, and the vigorous growth habit. But if you need a hardy rose for a difficult spot, 'Blanc Double de Coubert' is a spectacular choice.

'Blaze'

('Improved Blaze')

TYPE/CLASS: climber

HEIGHT: 7–9 feet (2–2.7m)
or more

BLOOM SIZE: 2½–3 inches (6.5–7.5cm)

BLOOM TIME: repeats all summer

FRAGRANCE: slight

'Blaze'

Ablaze with bloom for practically the whole summer, this fabulous climber has generous clusters of big flowers. They're more cherry red than crimson, full of petals, and tend to open all at once—so each spray looks like its own festive bouquet. Unlike some other climbers, 'Blaze' produces blooms along its entire length, which makes it especially suitable for high-traffic areas where it can be admired close at hand.

The plant itself is a vigorous grower, eagerly mounting whatever support you provide it. Its leaves are medium green and disease-resistant. A real prize, this exuberant and trouble-free rose is easy and satisfying to grow. Plants labeled 'Improved Blaze' are touted as extra-disease-resistant.

'Bonica'

('Bonica '82')

TYPE/CLASS: shrub

HEIGHT: 2–4 feet (60–120cm) or more

BLOOM SIZE: 1–2½ inches (2.5–6.5cm)

BLOOM TIME: repeats all summer

FRAGRANCE: none

'Bonica'

Before 1987, no shrub rose had ever won an All-America Rose Selection award, but this one swept the competition that year. It has long, arching branches that are often completely covered by wide sprays of small, full, delicate pink blooms. The leaves are also diminutive and generally disease-free.

But the bush is hardly dainty. It is tough as nails, enduring hot summers and cold winters with equal aplomb.

'Bonica' naturally maintains a compact habit, and asks little from the gardener. It might be the perfect rose if you need a tallish cover for an embankment, but it's also pretty enough to merit a spot in the garden proper. (Note: To avoid confusion with an earlier, obscure rose of the same name, some suppliers use the name 'Bonica '82'.)

'Brandy'

TYPE/CLASS: hybrid tea

HEIGHT: 4–5 feet (1.2–1.5m)

BLOOM SIZE: 4–5 inches (10–13cm)

BLOOM TIME: repeats all summer

FRAGRANCE: strong

'Brandy'

An elegant and perfectly formed rose, the aptly named 'Brandy' has blossoms in a unique shade of coppery apricot, which is a little darker on the interior of the petals than on the outside. Their fragrance is sweet yet slightly spicy, like that of orange blossoms. The leaves have a touch of mahogany to them, especially when new, which makes a gorgeous counterpart to the flowers.

The plant is a strong grower, with a vaselike profile, and bears these wondrous blooms on long cutting stems. Its only flaw seems to be that it is not very winter hardy, but gardeners north of Zone 6 can nurse it through with diligent mulching and wrapping. For a stunning effect, try growing 'Brandy' in the company of white-flowered perennials, such as certain foxgloves or campanulas.

'Brass Band'

TYPE/CLASS: floribunda

HEIGHT: 3–3½ feet (90–105cm)

BLOOM SIZE: 3½–4 inches (8–10cm)

BLOOM TIME: repeats all summer

FRAGRANCE: medium

'Brass Band'

This sprightly rose took top honors in All-America Rose Selections in 1995, and it's easy to see why. A 'Brass Band' bush in full bloom is downright vivacious with bright color. And close inspection reveals that the individual flowers are also splendid. Like all floribundas, this one blooms in clusters, displaying everything from sunny yellow buds to partially open apricot-coral flowers, to fully open showpieces of orange-pink enriched with undertones of coral-pink. The petals are slightly scalloped and substantial, so they keep very well on the bush and are long-lasting in bouquets.

The plant is of top quality, too, with loads of glossy green leaves borne on a compact, somewhat mounding bush. Add 'Brass Band' to a border that features other bright flowers, or plant this shrub in groups for clouds of glorious color.

'Carefree Wonder'

TYPE/CLASS: shrub

HEIGHT: 3–5 feet (1–1.5m)

BLOOM SIZE: 4 inches (10cm)

BLOOM TIME: repeats all summer

FRAGRANCE: slight

'Carefree Wonder'

Admittedly, 'Carefree Wonder' is not the sexiest name, but it certainly is accurate. This plant is a classic example of the best a landscape rose can be: It grows vigorously in an upright yet casual shape, its fresh green foliage is impervious to disease, and it blooms abundantly throughout the summer. The small, perky flowers are a bright candied pink, with a creamy reverse, and are carried in sprays.

Perhaps the best use for this rugged rose would be in a long hedge. You probably won't have to spray it, but be sure to give it plenty of water and fertilizer so it will thrive.

'Chicago Peace'

TYPE/CLASS: hybrid tea

HEIGHT: 4½–5½ feet (1.3–1.5m)

BLOOM SIZE: 5–5½ inches (13–14cm)

BLOOM TIME: repeats all summer

FRAGRANCE: slight

'Chicago Peace'

A justly popular "sport," or chance mutation, of the famous 'Peace' rose, this one has all the best qualities of its parent, including lush, full-petaled blooms, a long bloom period, and a well-branched, husky habit. The main difference is in the flowers; these are decidedly livelier, more pink, and more ruffled. They're still a blend of colors, though, and you'll cherish the enriching tints of copper and the blossom's overall warm glow (thanks to yellow petal bases).

'Chicago Peace' is hardy (to Zone 6). Although its foliage is leathery and dark forest green, it does fall victim to blackspot, so if that disease is a problem in your area, you'll have to spray. Otherwise, it is a terrific rose, eager to please and adaptable to formal and informal garden schemes alike.

'Child's Play'

TYPE/CLASS: miniature

HEIGHT: 15–20 inches (38–51cm)

BLOOM SIZE: 1¾ inches (4.4cm)

BLOOM TIME: repeats all summer

FRAGRANCE: none

'Child's Play'

The first mini ever to sweep both the All-America Rose Selections and win an American Rose Society Award of Excellence (in 1993), this little charmer is as durable as it is pretty. The flowers are of exhibition quality, which means that they have the superb form of their larger cousins the hybrid teas, and that they keep well on the bush or in a vase. They're an unusual, enchanting color combination of crisp white with brushed-pink edges—small as they are, nobody will ever overlook them!

The plants display outstanding resistance to disease, and grow to their dwarf size full of crisp little leaves. Plant a row of 'Child's Play' in a deck planter for a real conversation piece, or tuck them into flower beds where their color will harmonize with the neighboring flowers.

'Chrysler Imperial'

TYPE/CLASS: hybrid tea

HEIGHT: 4–5 feet (1.2–1.5m)

BLOOM SIZE: 4½–5 inches (11–13cm)

BLOOM TIME: repeats all summer

FRAGRANCE: strong

'Chrysler Imperial'

Nowadays, probably no one would name a rose after a car. But when this one appeared in the early 1950s, Americans were in love with automobiles, and 'Chrysler Imperial' immediately conferred a certain panache and romance. The blooms are fabulous, in a rich, velvety shade of crimson, and they perfume the air with an irresistible, almost tangy orange scent. Prior to opening (at the stage when you'll probably want to cut some), the long, strong stems bear shapely, pointed buds. The plant blooms profusely, so you shouldn't hesitate to use your clippers!

The bush is upright yet compact, and laden with matte-green leaves. 'Chrysler Imperial' isn't without its flaws, but for years it remained a sentimental favorite, winning an All-America Selections Award and an award for its fragrance. Its main weakness is its susceptibility to mildew, so gardeners who live in damp climates may have to forego growing it (though it can tolerate humidity). Hot summers are best because the blossoms will open completely.

'Climbing Cécile Brünner'

TYPE/CLASS: climber

HEIGHT: 15–20 feet (4.6–6m)

BLOOM SIZE: 1½ inches (4cm)

BLOOM TIME: repeats all summer

FRAGRANCE: slight

'Climbing Cécile Brünner'

A climbing version of the immensely popular "sweetheart rose" (used so often in corsages and boutonnieres), this special plant has a lot to recommend it. The adorable pastel pink flowers are perfect, tiny versions of hybrid teas, lightly but sweetly scented, and carried in generous sprays. The plant blooms well in early summer, and continues on and off for months until cold weather stops it. Unlike some climbers, the canes aren't very thorny, which makes them easy to work with if you're training the rose on a large trellis, archway, or wall.

'Climbing Cécile Brünner' has demonstrated an ability to perform well in average to poor soil and to tolerate partial shade. So if you're seeking a large, yet delicate-looking climber, and don't have the best conditions to offer, this sweetheart may be your rose.

'Complicata'

TYPE/CLASS: shrub (gallica)

HEIGHT: 5–10 feet (1.5–3m)
   or more

BLOOM SIZE: 4–4½ inches (10–11cm)

BLOOM TIME: once, early summer

FRAGRANCE: medium

'Complicata'

A hybrid that hails from an ancient tribe of European roses, most of which are pink and all of which are fragrant, 'Complicata' is perhaps the best of the old-fashioned gallicas. Its blossoms are large yet single (only five petals) and a brilliant shade of pink, creamy white toward the center, and accented with a dainty boss of small yellow stamens. The scent is reminiscent of ripe berries, and the petals are treasured for potpourris and sachets because the fragrance keeps so well even when they're dried.

The foliage is a paler shade of green than the leaves of most roses, but it complements the flowers well. 'Complicata' is, however, vulnerable to mildew, so gardeners in damp climates beware. The plant is an enthusiastic grower, and will cause you less frustration if you grant it room to roam—it might make a good hedge along a back fence, for instance.

'Constance Spry'

TYPE/CLASS: English shrub

HEIGHT: 5–10 feet (1.5–3m)

BLOOM SIZE: 4½–5 inches (11–13cm)

BLOOM TIME: once in early summer

FRAGRANCE: strong

'Constance Spry'

This pure pink rose is famous thanks to one gorgeous, much-photographed specimen that drapes over a wall and around an elegant white wooden bench in the renowned rose garden at Mottisfont Abbey in Hampshire, England. As that display hints, 'Constance Spry' is a large rose, so while you don't necessarily need the white bench in order to grow it, you will certainly need plenty of space.

It is also famous among rosarians because it is a parent of David Austin's English roses. It has the same wonderful, huge, petal-laden blossoms that look almost like double peonies. Alas, however, the blooms of 'Constance Spry' appear only once a summer (while its successors repeat their bloom). The bloom period is long, though, and the fragrance is utterly luscious.

'Country Dancer'

TYPE/CLASS: shrub

HEIGHT: 4½ feet (1.3m)

BLOOM SIZE: 4 inches (10cm)

BLOOM TIME: repeats all summer

FRAGRANCE: medium

'Country Dancer'

'Country Dancer' was bred at Iowa State University by Griffith Buck, who dedicated years to developing what he and many others consider ideal roses: long-blooming, disease-resistant, and cold-hardy. Its toughness is indisputable, and sure to make this rose very popular with gardeners in the Midwest and North. But its beauty is a wonderful plus: the blooms are a vibrant watermelon pink, and full (but not overfull) of petals, somewhat resembling a double camellia flower. The fragrance is pleasantly fruity.

This is a vigorous shrub, growing taller than wide, so you'll find it easy to tuck in toward the back of a flower border. Just remember that it is constantly in bloom, so place it among companions that are flattered by the bright pink flowers.

'Cupcake'

TYPE/CLASS: miniatures

HEIGHT: 12–16 inches (30–40cm)

BLOOM SIZE: 1½ inches (4cm)

BLOOM TIME: repeats all summer

FRAGRANCE: none

'Cupcake'

Actually, this lovely little rose looks for all the world like the frosting roses found on wedding cakes. Borne in small clusters, each bloom is symmetrical, neat, and dainty, in a clear shade of pink that strays neither to white nor to rose. The petals are heavily textured, so they last well on the bush or when cut.

The bush is compact and covered with glossy green leaves. The stems are fairly thornless, which is another agreeable feature of this endearing plant. 'Cupcake' won a well-deserved Award of Excellence from the American Rose Society in 1983.

'Don Juan'

TYPE/CLASS: climber

HEIGHT: 8–10 feet (2.4–3m)

BLOOM SIZE: 4½–5 inches (11–13cm)

BLOOM TIME: repeats all summer

FRAGRANCE: strong

'Don Juan'

If you live in an area with relatively mild winters (Zones 8 and south), you will find no finer red climber than 'Don Juan'. Gardeners farther north who simply *must* have this rose may be able to get it through the cold weather by gingerly detaching the canes from their support, laying them along the ground, and mounding a mulch of soil and hay over the entire plant until spring returns.

As compared to the cherry red blossoms of the climber 'Blaze', these are a passionate, velvety crimson. With a classic hybrid tea shape, most blooms appear in clusters, but some are on single stems. The fragrance is heady, tawny, almost musky—enough to make you swoon! The dark, leathery leaves are disease-resistant. 'Don Juan' makes a spectacular pillar-trained specimen.

'Dortmund'

TYPE/CLASS: climber

HEIGHT: 10–30 feet (3–9m)

BLOOM SIZE: 3–3½ inches (7.5–8cm)

BLOOM TIME: repeats all summer

FRAGRANCE: medium

'Dortmund'

A super-hardy climber (to Zone 4), 'Dortmund' has been around for years, and has certainly stood the test of time. The flowers are single (they have just five petals), bright red, and glow in the center with a white eye. The petal edges are slightly scalloped, which lends a touch of welcome fancy. Handsome orange-red hips follow the blooms, but you ought to deadhead before they appear or clip them off early to encourage the plant to continue its profuse blooming a little longer. The foliage is quite dark and glossy, providing a nice contrast to both blooms and fruits.

This vigorous climber would be an appropriate accent in a garden of old-fashioned flowers because it has a nice, unpretentious charm. After one initially heavy bloom period, it repeats reliably for the rest of the summer. Only one caveat: without pruning, it may become rather big and sprawling.

'Double Delight'

TYPE/CLASS: hybrid tea

HEIGHT: 3½–4 feet (1–1.2m)

BLOOM SIZE: 5½ inches (14cm)

BLOOM TIME: repeats all summer

FRAGRANCE: strong

'Double Delight'

There is no other hybrid tea quite like 'Double Delight'. Winning raves from gardeners for years, it took top All-America Selections honors in 1977. The big blooms display unusual and spectacular coloration: The scarlet bud whirls open to a creamy white-washed pink blossom, ending in buttery yellow and strawberry red. (The amount of red seems to vary according to the weather.) The powerful scent is ravishing: rich, spicy, and fruity. Needless to say, these flowers make for superb bouquets. Pick them early in the opening process so you can savor the show indoors. As for fitting this unique rose into the garden, well, frankly, it's not easily paired with other roses or many other flowers. But after you've been smitten, you'll find a way.

Be forewarned that 'Double Delight' is a slow starter. It comes into full glory in its second and third seasons. Also, the medium green foliage is prone to mildew in damp climates, so spraying will be necessary for gardeners in those areas.

'Dreamglo'

TYPE/CLASS: miniature

HEIGHT: 18–24 inches (45–60cm)

BLOOM SIZE: 1 inch (2.5cm)

BLOOM TIME: repeats all summer

FRAGRANCE: slight

'Dreamglo'

The blooms of 'Dreamglo' are bicolor, with creamy white petals edged in rosy red, and are prized because they do not fade or wash out in the heat of summer. They have a formal, hybrid tea form, which means that they unfurl evenly from a high center. The overall impression is of a carefully crafted miniature ceramic replica of a rose. Not surprisingly, it is a favorite of rose aficionados who exhibit. The accompanying leaves are medium green, somewhat glossy, and moderately disease-resistant.

On the tall side for a miniature, this vigorous plant easily reaches a height of 2 feet (60cm) so it would be a nice choice for a border along the front of the house, or following a walkway. Winter protection is recommended north of Zone 7.

'Dublin Bay'

TYPE/CLASS: climber

HEIGHT: 8–14 feet (2.4–4.2m)

BLOOM SIZE: 4½ inches (11cm)

BLOOM TIME: repeats all summer

FRAGRANCE: medium

'Dublin Bay'

An excellent climber, this rose has everything going for it. Its deep red flowers are big but not blowsy and double-petaled but not overfull. They appear in loose clusters, so a plant in full bloom is literally clothed in flowers. The large, handsome, leathery leaves are disease-resistant. Growing vigorously but not rampantly, the stems are only moderately thorny, and are easily trained on anything from a pillar to a trellis.

The plant tends to have a lush blooming in early to mid-summer. But since it continues to pump out a steady parade of quality blooms, it won't disappoint through the rest of the season. 'Dublin Bay' is a particular favorite of gardeners in the damp Pacific Northwest because its buds and flowers still look great even if it's been raining on and off all week.

'Europeana'

TYPE/CLASS: floribunda

HEIGHT: 2½–3 feet (75–90cm)

BLOOM SIZE: 3 inches (7.5cm)

BLOOM TIME: repeats all summer

FRAGRANCE: slight

'Europeana'

As an alternative red rose to the generally one-to-a-stem hybrid teas, the cluster-blooming 'Europeana' can't be beat. In any given spray, you'll find the handsome flowers in all stages of development. The stout buds are a classic crimson; they open to reveal medium-size, cupped flowers in a fancy ruby red hue that holds its color well.

This low, spreading shrub also owes its enduring appeal to its foliage, which starts out mahogany (a beautiful backdrop for the blooms) and eventually goes to a rich dark green. It won an All-America Selections award in 1968.

Tall, commanding red hybrid teas are not always easy to place in the garden. Because of its generous sprays of flowers, 'Europeana' is more obliging, particularly if your flower borders include a range of perennials and annuals. It doesn't take up much space, it blooms dependably, and it flatters other bright colors. The only complaint made about 'Europeana' is its occasional bouts with mildew; good air circulation and spraying will prevent that.

'Fair Bianca'

TYPE/CLASS: English shrub

HEIGHT: 3 feet (1m)

BLOOM SIZE: 3–3½ inches (7.5-8cm)

BLOOM TIME: repeats all summer

FRAGRANCE: strong

'Fair Bianca'

It's hard to imagine a prettier, more romantic rose. The stout, round buds are rosy pink, but open to a very lush, symmetrically arranged creamy white blossom. Both stages of bloom are on the bush at any given time, and the effect is adorable. As for the fragrance, it is intense and reminiscent of anise—not too sweet. You won't be able to resist picking bouquets for the house, and you'll be pleased to see that these roses have a long vase life.

Most of the David Austin English roses are medium to large plants; this one is small and compact, ideal for a smaller garden or incorporating into a flower bed. Still, the bush maintains a graceful upright habit. The foliage is matte green and not very dense, lending this rose an overall lacy effect.

'The Fairy'

TYPE/CLASS: shrub (polyantha)

HEIGHT: 1 ½–3 feet (45–90cm)

BLOOM SIZE: 1–1 ½ inches (2.5–4cm)

BLOOM TIME: repeats all summer

FRAGRANCE: none

'The Fairy'

Visitors to your garden might not realize, at first glance, that this is a rose. 'The Fairy' is unique. The adorable pink flowers are tiny, round, and so fluffy with petals that you could almost take them for itsy-bitsy peony blooms. They're borne on abundant sprays that emerge from the equally diminutive shiny green leaves. Blooming occurs a little later than other roses, but the show is certainly in full swing by midsummer, and it doesn't quit until the cold weather comes.

Speaking of cold weather, 'The Fairy' is also exceptionally hardy. It can be grown, and grown well, as far north as Zone 4. And thanks to its unusual appearance, it neither requires nor especially benefits from being grown in a traditional rose garden. This rose really fits in beautifully in a perennial border. It will billow around its companions as they go in and out of bloom, and offer a pretty counterpart to everything from mound-forming blue campanulas to spiky white or purple veronicas.

There seems to be a natural variability in this rose, or perhaps alternate versions are on the market. It can be found as a low, sprawling near-groundcover and as a more upright, though not tall, bush.

'First Prize'

TYPE/CLASS: hybrid tea

HEIGHT: 4–5 feet (1.2–1.5m)

BLOOM SIZE: 5–5½ inches (13–14cm)

BLOOM TIME: repeats all summer

FRAGRANCE: slight

'First Prize'

As the name suggests, this rose has won many awards, including All-America Selections in 1970. The lovely, unique blooms are big, pleasantly scented, and meet the rose aficionado's standard of perfect form. They begin as long, ivory buds but spiral open to reveal a painterly shade of medium pink (almost as if they'd been touched with an artist's brush). This gradually flushes on the outer edges to a richer rose color. The original ivory remains to lighten the very center of the bloom. A fully open flower is a breathtaking sight. Like most hybrid teas, 'First Prize' has nice long stems, ideal for cutting—you'll want to pick some just as the buds are beginning to unfurl so you can savor the full effect.

The leaves are dark and leathery, but, alas, not immune to disease. Mildew and blackspot are often a problem. Yet the bush grows vigorously and continues to bloom on and off all summer. It is not especially hardy, so is best enjoyed by gardeners in Zones 7 and south.

'Flower Carpet'

TYPE/CLASS: groundcover

HEIGHT: 1 foot (30cm)

BLOOM SIZE: 2–3 inches (5–7.5cm)

BLOOM TIME: repeats all summer

FRAGRANCE: none

'Flower Carpet'

This rose, officially introduced to North America in 1990, is still quite new. Although the jury's still out, it certainly looks terrific—you'll find it showcased at many garden centers these days. It is marketed as hardy and extra tough, and is touted as tolerating all soil types, even clay. It is also billed as "the environmental rose," meaning that the dark green, glossy foliage should remain healthy and does not require spraying.

But the most remarkable quality of 'Flower Carpet' is its profuse blooms: it foams with clusters of pretty, dark pink blooms for months on end. So if you use it as a groundcover, you can count on a big sweep of color. It would also be an exuberant container plant. In any event, watch for this unique newcomer to grow in popularity—and, no doubt, for more color options to appear in the near future.

'Fragrant Cloud'

TYPE/CLASS: hybrid tea

HEIGHT: 3–5 feet (1–1.5m)

BLOOM SIZE: 4–5 inches (10–13cm)

BLOOM TIME: repeats all summer

FRAGRANCE: strong

'Fragrant Cloud'

The old phrase about 'Fragrant Cloud' is true: "One bloom can scent an entire room!" Indeed, this rose has won many awards for its fragrance, including the prestigious Gamble medal. Rich and intoxicating, it smells of tangerine and mandarin orange.

The blossom's color is the perfect complement to its fabulous fragrance. A pure coral-red from petal tip to petal base, it is simply gorgeous. The large bloom size also adds to the impact (unlike some hybrid teas, it blooms in clus-ters). And you can expect a steady parade of blooms throughout the summer.

All this splendor is borne on an upright bush of luxuri-ous, dark green foliage that resists disease. The plant is also winter-hardy to Zone 7 at least. Give it a prominent spot in your garden and bring your clippers when you're showing it off, so you can send visitors home with a memo-rable bouquet.

'French Lace'

TYPE/CLASS: floribunda

HEIGHT: 3–3½ feet (90–105cm)

BLOOM SIZE: 3½–4 inches (8–10cm)

BLOOM TIME: repeats all summer

FRAGRANCE: medium

'French Lace'

Neither white nor pink, but falling in some sweet, romantic spot between the two, 'French Lace' is an utterly captivating rose. It bears clusters of three to twelve buds, which are ivory to light apricot. The flowers open to porcelain-perfect ivory blooms blushed with a soft pink glow. The blooms are full of petals, giving them an endearing old-fashioned look. Hot sun releases their delicate, carnationlike fragrance.

The dark, smallish leaves (which are rarely troubled by disease) and the thin but strong stems give the bush a lacy look. 'French Lace' grows taller than most floribundas, and combines well with pastel-colored cottage-garden flowers. Not super-hardy, it should be protected for the winter months if you garden in Zones 7 and north. This rose was bestowed with top All-America Selections honors in 1982.

'Fru Dagmar Hastrup'
('Frau Dagmar Hartopp')

TYPE/CLASS: rugosa hybrid

HEIGHT: 3–4 feet (90–120cm)

BLOOM SIZE: 3–3½ inches (7.5–8cm)

BLOOM TIME: repeats all summer

FRAGRANCE: strong

'Fru Dagmar Hastrup'

Considered by some rosarians to be a classic among rugosas, this older variety (bred in Denmark in 1914) has many virtues. In addition to the winter hardiness and immunity to disease we've come to expect from rugosas, this one has especially enchanting blooms. They're large and single, with nearly white stamens, but open cupped rather than flat, which gives them a more refined look. Petal color is beautiful: a soft, elegant, pewter-tinted pink with darker pink veins, almost reminiscent of a geranium petal.

Plus, they're fragrant, smelling strongly of spice. The blooms literally envelop the plant for most of the summer— an unbeatable performance. And in the autumn, look forward to a showing of large, bright red hips.

Possessed of a tidier, better-mannered growth habit than some of its peers, this rose might be the perfect candidate for a low hedge or a property-line planting. Just be warned, 'Fru Dagmar Hastrup' is very thorny.

'Gold Medal'

TYPE/CLASS: grandiflora

HEIGHT: 4½–5½ feet (1.3–1.6m)

BLOOM SIZE: 4 inches (10cm)

BLOOM TIME: repeats all summer

FRAGRANCE: slight

'Gold Medal'

A real powerhouse of big blooms all summer long, 'Gold Medal' flowers in clusters like a floribunda. The difference is that grandifloras tend to open all their flowers at once, so you get quite a blast of color. And what color! A rich, enduring butter yellow, their edges are touched with orange or, in some cases, red, which helps to define their size and beauty from a distance. The blooms of 'Gold Medal' sport a slight, pleasing, citrusy fragrance. They are at their best in warm climates.

A tall, vigorous plant, you can expect a dependable performance from it year after year. It is generally the picture of health, although occasionally it suffers from blackspot.

'Gourmet Popcorn'

TYPE/CLASS: miniature

HEIGHT: 24 inches (60cm)

BLOOM SIZE: 1 inch (2.5cm)

BLOOM TIME: repeats all summer

FRAGRANCE: none

'Gourmet Popcorn'

'Gourmet Popcorn' has been called "the most popular miniature in America," and no wonder. The flowers, carried in generous clusters, are absolutely irresistible, with a double complement of fluttery white petals centered by butter yellow stamens. The tiny buds are also yellow. So at any given time over the course of the summer, the bush is alive with fresh, spunky color—it was given the perfect name!

On the tall side for a miniature, the bush is also of high quality. The small leaves are a flattering shade of dark green, tough, and disease-resistant. The stems have a pleasant cascading habit that further showcases the wonderful blossoms. Give this plant a prominent spot, or devote an entire bed or row to it. It is sure to be a constant source of delight.

'Graham Thomas'

TYPE/CLASS: English shrub

HEIGHT: 4–6 feet (1.2–1.8m) or more

BLOOM SIZE: 3½–4 inches (8–10cm)

BLOOM TIME: repeats all summer

FRAGRANCE: strong

'Graham Thomas'

The most striking thing about this outstandingly beautiful rose is its golden yellow color, too rarely seen in old or new roses. Bred by David Austin, it is quite a tribute to the venerable English rosarian for whom it was named. The cupped flowers are very full, have a generous, tea rose scent, and bloom in clusters. Against a backdrop of matte green leaves, the blooms are completely charming. 'Graham Thomas' always puts forth a great shower of blooms in early summer.

It usually repeats well in most areas (especially those with hot summers) throughout the ensuing months.

The bush is a vigorous grower, and can become fairly tall. Some gardeners have even successfully trained it as a climber. In any event, if your taste runs to the old-fashioned, cottage-garden look, this rose is an absolute must. It is splendid among billowing perennials, especially those with blue or purple flowers.

'Granada'

TYPE/CLASS: hybrid tea

HEIGHT: 5–6 feet (1.5–1.8m)

BLOOM SIZE: 4–5 inches (10–13cm)

BLOOM TIME: repeats all season

FRAGRANCE: strong

'Granada'

There is something wonderfully festive about the deeply fragrant blossoms of this fine rose. A rich blend of dark pink, light pink, and glowing yellow, they seem to be bursting with eager energy. They are smaller than many hybrid tea flowers, but that hardly detracts from their appeal. 'Granada' is a prolific bloomer, and has long cutting stems. You'll find both single-flower stems and the occasional cluster. This rose can fit into various spots in a garden, complementing yellow flowers or contributing its multi-shaded pinks to a pastel-themed border.

The bush has nice, dark, leathery leaves, an upright habit, and is pretty thorny. It is susceptible to mildew, which is best headed off by preventative spraying. 'Granada' is not especially hardy, and does best in Zones 7 and south. It tends to bloom earlier than most roses, and may well become your season-starter.

'Handel'

TYPE/CLASS: climber

HEIGHT: 12–15 feet (3.7–4.6m)

BLOOM SIZE: 3½ inches (8cm)

BLOOM TIME: repeats all summer

FRAGRANCE: none to slight

'Handel'

A classically beautiful bicolor climber, 'Handel' has amazing flowers. Not only are they perfectly formed doubles (that is, displaying upwards of two dozen petals per bloom), but their color is flawless: pure creamy white, gently edged with rose pink. Their debut in midsummer is especially lush, but the plant always repeats on and off for the rest of the season. The fragrance, most detectable on a hot summer day, is softly fruity. Foliage is glossy and medium olive green. Blackspot can be a problem.

'Handel' is a vigorous climber, and you can count on it to cover any support you choose. Its elegant flowers look best in a formal garden setting. Try it on a fan-shaped or lattice trellis, or on a wrought-iron archway.

'Hansa'

TYPE/CLASS: rugosa hybrid

HEIGHT: 4–8 feet (1.2–2.4m)

BLOOM SIZE: 3–3½ inches (7.5–8cm)

BLOOM TIME: repeats all summer

FRAGRANCE: strong

'Hansa'

A very old rugosa hedge rose, still beloved for its rich color, 'Hansa' remains unmatched by any modern relative. The splendid purplish-crimson blooms are reminiscent of the color of a fine Zinfandel wine (though in hot weather, it subsides to lavender). Unlike some rugosas, the flowers are fluffy, full-petaled doubles. And its scent is powerfully spicy. Unfortunately, the stems are too short and weak to make good bouquets. 'Hansa' puts on a great show in spring, repeats periodically through the ensuing months, and finally yields to a full display of large, scarlet hips in autumn.

The remarkably colored blooms are well set off by dark, disease-free foliage. The plants tend to grow as wide as they are tall, a desirable quality in a hedge. If the fresh, vibrant color combination does not clash with your house color or garden scheme, 'Hansa' makes a vigorous boundary or streetside planting.

'Henry Hudson'

TYPE/CLASS: rugosa hybrid

HEIGHT: 3 feet (90cm)

BLOOM SIZE: 3–4 inches (7.5–10cm)

BLOOM TIME: repeats all summer

FRAGRANCE: medium

'Henry Hudson'

One of the newer rugosa varieties, 'Henry Hudson' is part of the Explorer series produced in Canada, so you can count on its hardiness (to Zone 4 at least). It's a dense plant and doesn't grow as tall or wide as some others, which makes it ideal for a low border or hedge in a smaller yard. If you want it to acheive its maximum height, find a spot where it gets less sun—it will grow up to a foot (30cm) taller.

The flowers are lovely. They begin as chubby, deep pink buds and burst open to almost flattened, creamy white blooms with plenty of fluffy petals and a bright center of golden stamens. Cooler temperatures cause them to flush slightly pink. The fragrance is not as overpowering as some rugosas, but still has that signature spiciness. The only shortcoming in this otherwise superb plant is that the flowers must be deadheaded; if you leave them on the rose, they shrivel up, turn brown, and detract from the plant's beauty.

'Heritage'

TYPE/CLASS: English shrub

HEIGHT: 4–6 feet (1.2–1.8m)

BLOOM SIZE: 4–5 inches (10–13cm)

BLOOM TIME: repeats all summer

FRAGRANCE: strong

'Heritage'

This perfectly gorgeous, pure pink rose is destined to become a classic. Its breeder, the esteemed David Austin, says it's his favorite—quite a statement, considering how many lovely English roses he has developed! The blooms are dense with shell pink petals, cup-shaped, and waft a seductive, lemon tea fragrance into the air. They're carried in sprays, which makes the bush's prolific performance all the more generous.

The plant is also of excellent quality. Neither too large nor too small, it has a handsome, compact habit that recommends it for single plantings as well as group shows. While not completely thornless, the canes are far less bristly than some English roses. It is also more winter-hardy than some of its relatives.

'*Honor*'

TYPE/CLASS: hybrid tea

HEIGHT: 5–7 feet (1.5–2m)

BLOOM SIZE: 4–5 inches (10–13cm)

BLOOM TIME: repeats all summer

FRAGRANCE: slight

'Honor'

There may be other white hybrid teas, but 'Honor' is a stand-out. The color is an exceptionally pure, sugared white, tending neither toward soft pink nor cream or yellow. The buds on this relentless bloomer are big and stately, and unfurl to large, double blooms that flatten out to almost a saucer shape without losing their grace. And the cutting stems are especially long. White roses aren't generally very fragrant, but you will detect a sweet, delicate scent that suits the plant's cool, soothing demeanor.

Meanwhile, the dark, glossy foliage is fairly large, in scale with the blooms. Usually quite healthy, it is occasionally troubled by mildew later in the season. The plant's habit is upright and vigorous. With these many sterling qualities, it comes as no surprise that 'Honor' is an award-winner. The All-America Rose Selections hailed it upon its introduction in 1980. If you have a white house or fence, this rose is a must.

'Iceberg'

TYPE/CLASS: floribunda

HEIGHT: 3–4 feet (90–120cm)

BLOOM SIZE: 3 inches (7.5cm)

BLOOM TIME: repeats all summer

FRAGRANCE: medium

'Iceberg'

Justly popular for almost forty years, this sweetly scented floribunda is unrivaled for its fast yet neat growth and its glorious sprays of flowers. Each spray is composed of up to a dozen blooms in various stages of opening. And at all stages, the full-petaled flowers retain their wondrous, crisp whiteness. You'll want to be out harvesting flowers for bouquets all the time, which is fine, because 'Iceberg' is an enthusiastic bloomer and will quickly replenish the supply.

A robust plant, it is enveloped in attractive, smallish light green leaves and is practically thorn-free. Admirably impervious to disease, it is vulnerable only to blackspot in areas where this disease is traditionally a problem (spraying should take care of that, though). Because 'Iceberg' is somewhat taller than other floribundas, you can spotlight it as a specimen plant. Try a pair flanking a gate or doorway, where their beauty, fragrance, and near-thornlessness will be much admired.

'Ingrid Bergman'

TYPE/CLASS: hybrid tea

HEIGHT: 4 ½ feet (1.3m)

BLOOM SIZE: 4–5 inches (10–13cm)

BLOOM TIME: repeats all summer

FRAGRANCE: none

'Ingrid Bergman'

'Ingrid Bergman' is perhaps the most popular red rose in Europe, and is slowly catching on in North America. It has won numerous awards in Europe, including gold medals at competitions in Madrid and Belfast and top honors in The Hague (note the diverse climates!).

As classy as the actress it is named for, 'Ingrid Bergman' features immaculate, silky blooms of deep, dark red. These hold up remarkably well in the heat of summer, without the wilting or burned edges that some of its peers are prone to. They're carried on long cutting stems, and can last for quite a while in a vase. The dense foliage is a rich, dark green. The plant's only flaw is that it lacks fragrance. Otherwise, there is probably no finer red bedding rose anywhere.

'Intrigue'

TYPE/CLASS: floribunda

HEIGHT: 3 feet (90cm)

BLOOM SIZE: 3 inches (7.5cm)

BLOOM TIME: repeats all summer

FRAGRANCE: strong

'Intrigue'

If you adore fragrant roses, award-winning 'Intrigue' is a stunning choice. A heady, delicious, almost lemony scent literally radiates from this bush on hot summer days. And the color is a knockout: a rich, deep plum, rare in floribundas—and indeed in all roses. The petals are especially ruffled, giving the blooms an almost old-fashioned look.

Like all floribundas, this rose blooms in clusters, so the bush is frequently laden with color. Dark green, leathery leaves complete the picture. It is no wonder 'Intrigue' has many fans; its awards include the coveted Fragrance Medal at Madrid and All-America honors in 1984.

The compact bush habit makes it easy to incorporate 'Intrigue' into the garden proper, perhaps in the heart of a sunny perennial border. As for color combinations, try it with white or pale yellow flowers—in the garden and in a vase.

'Jean Kenneally'

TYPE/CLASS: miniature

HEIGHT: 1½–2 feet (45–60cm) or more

BLOOM SIZE: 1½ inches (4cm)

BLOOM TIME: repeats all summer

FRAGRANCE: slight

'Jean Kenneally'

In 1986, this superb miniature won an Award of Excellence from the American Rose Society. It's easy to see why. Not only is it of "exhibition quality" (meaning flawless form and habit), but it makes a great landscaping rose, too. When well cared for, the handsome, upright bush grows taller and wider than most miniatures.

As for the flowers, they are irresistible. They're a sweet honeyed apricot color throughout, and have a classic, hybrid tea shape (though, of course, they're much smaller). Carried in lush clusters, they cover the bush when it blooms in midseason and repeat well for many weeks to follow.

If you have a pastel flower border, 'Jean Kenneally' is an appropriate size and color for inclusion. Or use it as an edging, down a row of taller roses.

'Jeeper's Creeper'

TYPE/CLASS: groundcover

HEIGHT: 2–2½ feet (60–75cm)

BLOOM SIZE: 1½ inches (4cm)

BLOOM TIME: repeats all summer

FRAGRANCE: none

'Jeeper's Creeper'

Groundcover roses are still a relatively new introduction, but since they're long-blooming, they're bound for wide popularity. 'Jeeper's Creeper' is probably the best white to appear so far. An incredibly heavy bloomer, it smothers its low, sprawling form with crisp white blossoms. These are single, open or loosely cupped, and display a sparkling center of yellow stamens. The leaves are correspondingly small and a nice, bright green. The overall effect is both vivacious and cooling.

This plant would be ideal as a low-maintenance foundation, bank, or curbside planting. Although it doesn't grow tall, it spreads vigorously to the sides. Allow each plant about 5 feet (1.5m) of room.

'John Cabot'

TYPE/CLASS: climber (kordesii)

HEIGHT: 8–10 feet (2.4–3m)

BLOOM SIZE: 3–4 inches (7.5–10cm)

BLOOM TIME: repeats all summer

FRAGRANCE: none

'John Cabot'

Incredible as it may sound, this husky climber is hardy to Zone 3. Many years in the making, it was bred in Ottawa, Canada, and is part of the heralded Explorer series of ultra-hardy roses. The stems are long and arching, best suited to trellising, although you could also keep it in bounds as a large shrub.

The full-petaled, semidouble blooms are rich, deep pink tending toward red—sometimes they display a hint of violet. The foliage is medium green and highly resistant to disease.

A plant this tough, vigorous, and attractive is an excellent choice for anyone gardening in a harsh climate. It shouldn't need winter protection, and summer will find it showing off its lovely blooms for up to ten consecutive weeks.

'Joseph's Coat'

TYPE/CLASS: climber

HEIGHT: 8–10 feet (2.4–3m)

BLOOM SIZE: 3–4 inches (7.5–10cm)

BLOOM TIME: repeats all summer

FRAGRANCE: slight

'Joseph's Coat'

The name for this rose is truly inspired, because it is quite possibly the most multicolored or chameleonlike of all roses. To call it a "red and yellow bicolor" is an oversimplification. The large flowers open boldly yellow with red flushes; they change over a day or two to orangey red, with rose toward the outside of the petals and ivory within; finally, they become a softer rosy red and the ivory mellows to creamy yellow. Since the plant blooms in clusters, this exciting show is constantly going on in all stages. It tends to have a block-buster first round of blooms, then repeats a bit on and off for the rest of the summer. Some say 'Joseph's Coat' has no fragrance, but in fact it has quite an appealing, if gentle, somewhat fruity scent.

Although it makes a fine climber, you can also allow it to go its own way, with minimal maintenance pruning, and enjoy it as an exuberant, large shrub. Either way, it is sure to bring dynamic energy to your garden.

'Just Joey'

TYPE/CLASS: hybrid tea

HEIGHT: 3–3½ feet (90–105cm)

BLOOM SIZE: 4–5 inches (10–13cm)

BLOOM TIME: repeats all summer

FRAGRANCE: strong

'Just Joey'

Despite its large blooms, 'Just Joey' never gives the impression of being bold or aggressive. The subtle flower color has a lot to do with this—it's a gorgeous shade of coppery apricot through and through. And the foliage, which is dark green and disease-resistant, is mahogany-tinted, making for an elegant counterpart. Also, the plant itself is not especially large or spreading. The fragrance is strong, delicious, and spicy.

Before you fall in love with this rose, however, be aware of its climatic limitations. Very hot summers, as in the Deep South, tend to cause sparse growth and inhibit flowering. But it's not super-hardy, either, so gardeners north of Zone 6 will have to give it winter protection and hope for the best. That said, it is still among the loveliest and most worthwhile of all soft-colored roses.

'L. D. Braithwaite'

TYPE/CLASS: English shrub

HEIGHT: 5–6 feet (1.5–1.8m)

BLOOM SIZE: 4–4¼ inches

BLOOM TIME: repeats all summer

FRAGRANCE: strong

'L. D. Braithwaite'

Here's another triumph from English rose breeder David Austin. This one is special because the deep crimson color is outstanding, and stays fast without fading as so many other reds are prone to do. The flower is loosely packed with richly fragrant petals that are displayed in a cup shape. When it is completely open, you will detect a flash of gold from the stamens in the center.

The shrub is on the large side, and eventually grows as wide as it is tall. Its dense, emerald green foliage flatters those magnificent blooms. Whether it is placed in front of a white wall, alongside a white fence, or at the back of a classic, warm-hued perennial border, you can be sure that 'L. D. Braithwaite' will bring a touch of glory to your garden or yard.

'Louise Odier'

TYPE/CLASS: shrub (Bourbon)

HEIGHT: 4½–5½ feet (1.3–1.6m)

BLOOM SIZE: 3½ inches (8cm)

BLOOM TIME: repeats all summer

FRAGRANCE: strong

'Louise Odier'

An enduringly popular Victorian-style rose, 'Louise Odier' is a sensational, full-petaled dark pink blessed with an intoxicating scent. Its nearly thorn-free canes sometimes bow under the weight of the bloom clusters. That quality, coupled with its graceful upright, vaselike shape (most other Bourbons are large shrubs), lend the entire plant a pretty, fountain-of-blooms profile. Feature this old-fashioned classic in a prominent spot with ample elbow room so you can savor its beauty.

Unlike some other vintage roses, this rose repeat-blooms well into autumn. The plant is quite vigorous and winter hardy to Zones 4 and 5. It is also disease-resistant.

'Madame Alfred Carrière'

TYPE/CLASS: climber (noisette)

HEIGHT: 10–15 feet (3–4.6m) or more

BLOOM SIZE: 2½–3 inches (6.5–7.5cm)

BLOOM TIME: repeats all summer

FRAGRANCE: medium

'Madame Alfred Carrière'

A vigorous, old-fashioned climber that blooms in plush clusters, 'Madame Alfred Carrière' sports some of the prettiest and most fragrant blossoms to be found on a white climber. They are laden with petals, and open to a lush, loose, exuberant form. The color has a porcelain quality, opening very pale pink and maturing to a shade more cream than pure white. It repeat blooms very reliably. And the tea rose scent is quite powerful, noticeable from several feet away and dizzying if you stick your nose right into a blossom.

This rose is a good choice for a spot where you want fast and abundant cover, such as on a pillar or even a wall. Unlike some others, it will tolerate partial shade. The long, strong stems are clothed in plenty of bright green leaves. It is reasonably hardy (to Zone 6, at least).

'Madame Isaac Pereire'

TYPE/CLASS: shrub (Bourbon)

HEIGHT: 5–7 feet (1.5–2m)

BLOOM SIZE: 3½–4 inches (8–10cm)

BLOOM TIME: repeats all summer

FRAGRANCE: strong

'Madame Isaac Pereire'

It is worth noting that of all roses, both old-fashioned and new, this is the one professional rosarians frequently call "the world's most fragrant rose." The full, almost peony-shaped flowers are a splendid raspberry pink and the scent is a sure match: it's fruity and intoxicating, like sun-warmed berry jam.

Like other Bourbon roses, 'Madame Isaac Pereire' has a big, spreading, billowy form, with plenty of moderately thorny branches. The foliage is thick, dark green, and disease-resistant. You can grow it as a full shrub or train it as a climber. Either way, it will oblige with a prolific initial bloom in midsummer and continue to throw off additional blooms well into autumn.

Obviously, this is not a rose for the fainthearted. But if you have space for only one big rose, and want a showpiece, grow this one.

'Magic Carpet'

TYPE/CLASS: groundcover

HEIGHT: 18 inches (45cm)

BLOOM SIZE: 2 inches (5cm)

BLOOM TIME: repeats all summer

FRAGRANCE: medium

'Magic Carpet'

If you're seeking a fragrant groundcovering rose, look no further. Like other lavender-colored roses, 'Magic Carpet' has a pleasant spicy scent. From a distance, the blooms are a soft lilac color, but up close, you'll notice more charming details—each tiny petal has an accenting splash of white and the flower is centered with golden stamens. Blooms are semidouble, each carrying approximately fifteen petals. The foliage is a sharp, dark green.

The plant spends its vigor growing outward rather than upward. It sprawls in all directions to between 3 and 4 feet (90 and 120cm), so be sure to plan for this eventual size. No special pruning is necessary. Diligent watering and fertilizing will guarantee a lush carpet. Because of the lovely fragrance, this groundcover deserves to be sited where you can appreciate it daily, such as along the front of the house or bordering a walkway.

'Magic Carrousel'

TYPE/CLASS: miniature

HEIGHT: 15–18 inches (38–45cm)

BLOOM SIZE: 2 inches (5cm)

BLOOM TIME: repeats all summer

FRAGRANCE: none

'Magic Carrousel'

Although the semidouble blooms are small, they pack quite a punch when they're fully open. Each petal is creamy white but evenly rimmed with bright pinkish red. The overall effect is formal, which no doubt is the reason 'Magic Carrousel' is a popular choice of florists for boutonnieres. It also won an Award of Excellence from the American Rose Society in 1975.

The plant is of equally high quality. It's clothed in disease-resistant, medium-green leaves. With enough room to spread out (that is, if you plant it in the ground rather than in a pot), this vigorous miniature may reach 30 inches (75cm) tall.

To get the most out of 'Magic Carrousel', plant it where the whiteness of the inner petals becomes an accent. Try a row along a white fence or wall, or near white-barked birch trees. Just make sure it doesn't get too much shade.

'Maiden's Blush'

TYPE/CLASS: shrub (alba)

HEIGHT: 5–8 feet (1.5–2.4m)

BLOOM SIZE: 3 inches (7.5cm)

BLOOM TIME: blooms once in early summer

FRAGRANCE: strong

'Maiden's Blush'

The combination of soft pastel blooms and soft-colored leaves on this old-fashioned shrub is unique and enchanting. Although "alba" means white, the loosely double blooms open shell pink and soften over several days until the center is the darkest part remaining and the outer petals are cream-colored. This lovely sight is displayed against profuse blue-gray foliage.

The plant only blooms once a season, but it does so abundantly. Borne in sprays, the flowers seem to froth out-ward on the graceful, arching canes. The tantalizing fragrance is not overwhelming, but lingers in your memory. By all means, cut some for bouquets—and display them in your most elegant vase.

A good way to use this distinctive rose is along the rear of a pastel-themed perennial border. The flowers will enhance the display when they are in bloom, and the foliage will remain through the rest of the season as an elegant, novel backdrop.

'Mary Rose'

TYPE/CLASS: English shrub

HEIGHT: 4–6 feet (1.2–1.8m)

BLOOM SIZE: 4 inches (10cm)

BLOOM TIME: repeats all summer

FRAGRANCE: medium

'Mary Rose'

Many rosarians agree that 'Mary Rose' is one of David Austin's finest English rose introductions. The plant's habit is simply outstanding: It grows strongly into a dense, well-branched, handsome bush that responds especially well to pruning (just watch out for the thorns!). 'Mary Rose' has also shown itself to be pest- and disease-resistant.

Meanwhile, the blooms are some of the most romantic you'll find anywhere. Gorgeous, full-petaled, and cupped, they're pure peppermint pink, redolent with sweet rose perfume. The plant starts blooming early in the season, and doesn't let up until autumn, a terrific performance. If you love the look of old-fashioned roses but want a full season of bloom, look no further than this sure classic.

'Medallion'

TYPE/CLASS: hybrid tea

HEIGHT: 4½–5½ feet (1.3–1.6m)

BLOOM SIZE: 5–7 inches (13–18cm)

BLOOM TIME: repeats all summer

FRAGRANCE: strong

'Medallion'

This rose's enormous flowers are dramatic from across a yard and enchanting at close range. The classically formed pink to crimson buds unfurl to silky, rose-blushed orange blossoms that mellow to light apricot. The plant is in bloom all summer long, and the fragrance is rich and fruity, like sun-warmed nectarines. Not surprisingly, this magnificent bloomer was an All-America Rose Selection in 1973, the year it was introduced.

These flowers make fantastic bouquets not only because of the long cutting stems but also because the petals gain longevity from their heavy texture. But wait until the bud is starting to spring open before cutting, or it may not finish.

Taller and more stately than many hybrid teas, 'Medallion' offers great presence in a garden, so don't place it too far back or out of range. Instead, try to find a spot where it can solo, such as a corner or entrance. This siting will also address the plant's only flaw—its large, medium-green foliage can get mildewed, and better air circulation will help. Also, north of Zone 7, be sure to give this rose winter protection.

'Mermaid'

TYPE/CLASS: climber

HEIGHT: 15–20 feet (4.6–6m)

BLOOM SIZE: 4½–5½ inches (11–14cm)

BLOOM TIME: once in midsummer

FRAGRANCE: medium

'Mermaid'

Single, cupped flowers of a sweet canary yellow cascade from this very vigorous climber. There are only five petals per blossom, but they are flawless, and made even lovelier by a generous flush of jewellike golden stamens in their centers. The fragrance is sweetly honeyed. 'Mermaid' always has a wonderful, long-lasting debut in midsummer, and in mild climates it often reblooms repeatedly for many weeks to follow.

The plant itself is anything but delicate. The dark green leaves are admirably disease-resistant. But the long, wickedly thorny stems are lax, somewhat brittle, and difficult to prune.

Given half a chance, 'Mermaid' will grow lustily and cover a large area, so the best sites for it are probably ones where you can leave it be. Let it smother a dead or dying tree, a tall fence, or an unattractive shed or other outbuilding. Finally, be aware that this rose is rather tender, and won't thrive north of Zone 7.

'Mister Lincoln'

TYPE/CLASS: hybrid tea

HEIGHT: 4½–5½ feet (1.3–1.6m)

BLOOM SIZE: 5½ inches (14cm)

BLOOM TIME: repeats all summer

FRAGRANCE: strong

'Mister Lincoln'

A big All-America Selections award-winner in 1965, no other red rose has held rose-lovers' affections so well for so long, and perhaps none ever will. A true classic, the 'Mister Lincoln' blossom is exactly what you dream of: richly colored, powerfully perfumed, and classically formed. The cutting stems are long and strong and each one bears a single flower. You may harvest it in the bud, but wait until the lower sepals have peeled back.

The plant itself is equally elegant. It is tallish, robust, and forms a lovely urn shape. The medium-green leaves are large and significantly more mildew-resistant than those of other red roses (though they are not immune). As for the bloom period, expect a long-running performance. Rather than flagging on hot summer days, 'Mister Lincoln' is sensational.

'Morden Blush'

TYPE/CLASS: shrub

HEIGHT: 2½–4 feet (75–120cm)

BLOOM SIZE: 3–4 inches

BLOOM TIME: repeats all summer

FRAGRANCE: none

'Morden Blush'

The surprising thing about this low-growing shrub is that it possesses such delicate beauty, yet is such a tough plant. Each picture-perfect, double blossom has lightly scalloped petals of softest peachy pink; these are carried in lush sprays. They're set against splendid, glossy, dark green foliage. A single bush would bring character to a flower border of comparable-size perennials, while a whole row would make a lovely hedge.

As for hardiness, 'Morden Blush' is hard to beat. Its Canadian breeders have found that it sails through Zone 3 winters. It also tolerates summer heat very well. And if all that wasn't enough, this excellent plant is also a workhorse of a bloomer. It's been known to bloom nonstop for three solid months.

'Morden Fireglow'

TYPECLASS: shrub

HEIGHT: 3–5 feet (1–1.5m)

BLOOM SIZE: 3 inches (7.5cm)

BLOOM TIME: repeats all summer

FRAGRANCE: none

'Morden Fireglow'

The aptly named 'Morden Fireglow' is another exceptionally hardy shrub rose (to Zone 3, at least) from the famous Canadian breeding program. The fully double blossoms are brilliantly colored—rich scarlet underlaid with a coral-orange glow, and are produced in sprays of up to five blossoms. The thick-textured petals stand up well to wind and weather, and last for a long time in flower arrangements.

Best of all, the blossoms are produced constantly for many weeks running.

Upright and full in habit, the shrub is covered in forest green, durable leaves. It's a vigorous grower, so if you're seeking an especially tough hedge or border rose in this color, you won't do any better than 'Morden Fireglow'.

'Nevada'

TYPE/CLASS: shrub

HEIGHT: 6–8 feet (1.8–2.4m)

BLOOM SIZE: 4 inches (10cm)

BLOOM TIME: repeats all summer

FRAGRANCE: none

'Nevada'

The single flowers of this graceful shrub look almost like Japanese anemone blossoms: they're saucer-shaped, rich, creamy white, and centered by a small spray of yellow stamens. In cool weather, they often develop a light pink tinge. Unusual for a shrub rose, but quite attractive, is the disease-resistant, small, light lime green foliage. The plant is an especially prolific bloomer, covering itself in blooms from head to toe for weeks on end. The flowers are followed in autumn by a scattering of orange hips.

Other good qualities of this unique rose are its low thorn count and handsome, arching red canes. 'Nevada' tends to grow as tall as it is wide, so be sure to allot it enough space. It would be a wonderful choice for a property-line hedge because no neighbor could ever fault its performance or agreeable color.

'New Dawn'

TYPE/CLASS: climber

HEIGHT: 12–20 feet (3.7–6m)

BLOOM SIZE: 3–3½ inches (7.5–8cm)

BLOOM TIME: repeats all summer

FRAGRANCE: medium

'New Dawn'

A sport, or mutant, of the famed 'Dr. W. Van Fleet', this splendid climber is deservedly popular. Starting out in a soft, cool, almost silvery shade of pink, the fluffy, cupped blossoms of 'New Dawn' gradually age to cream without losing their silky texture. They're centered with bright gold stamens. The sweet and fruity scent is especially enticing on hot summer afternoons. And you'll find that the glossy leaves are disease-resistant, especially to blackspot.

Not only is 'New Dawn' beautiful, it has all the qualities you could wish for in a climber. It blooms along its entire length, extravagantly at first, and persistently, on and off, for the rest of the season. The long canes are flexible and agreeable to training, whether you choose a pillar or wall. It is hardy to Zone 4. And the plant is vigorous, so you don't have to pamper it. The only strike against it is its notoriously sharp and plentiful thorns.

'Olympiad'

TYPE/CLASS: hybrid tea

HEIGHT: 4–5 feet (1.2–1.5m)

BLOOM SIZE: 4–4½ inches (10–11cm)

BLOOM TIME: repeats all summer

FRAGRANCE: none

'Olympiad'

For almost twenty years, no red rose was good enough to rival the wildly popular 'Mister Lincoln'. But in 1984, 'Olympiad' (named in honor of the Los Angeles Olympics) captured the All-America Selections award. It is prize-worthy for a few reasons. The blooms are as close to perfect as hybrid tea blooms get: they begin as elegant, pointed buds and spiral open to a clear, velvety scarlet that tends neither toward yellow nor lavender. And the color really holds—both on the bush, and in the vase. Most of the blooms are one-to-a-stem, and the stems (though fairly thorny) are admirably long and straight.

Another great feature of this rose is its exceptional mildew-resistance, which is good news for gardeners in areas with damp weather. The leaves are big, semiglossy, and medium green, and cover the plant well. As the great rosarian Peter Schneider laments, "if only it were fragrant, this might be the perfect rose."

'Party Girl'

TYPE/CLASS: miniature

HEIGHT: 12–16 inches (30–40cm)

BLOOM SIZE: 1¼ (3.5cm)

BLOOM TIME: repeats all summer

FRAGRANCE: medium

'Party Girl'

There are a number of perky yellow miniature roses around, but 'Party Girl' offers a softer, subtler alternative. Its blooms are light yellow-apricot, barely flushed with pink. They exhibit a double load of petals, but the form is not at all cluttered; the flowers open gracefully to a tiny version of a perfect hybrid tea. Unlike some minis, 'Party Girl' boasts blooms that are fragrant—the scent is warm and spicy. These enchanting flowers appear in clusters by the dozens at first flush, and continue on and off until the cold weather comes.

Rather than mounding, the small, vigorous plant develops an upright profile, so it would be ideal for disguising the bare knees of taller roses or other flowering shrubs. 'Party Girl' is also lovely in a pot. Either way, you should place it where its beauty can be appreciated at close range. It won an Award of Excellence from the American Rose Society in 1981.

'Pascali'

TYPE/CLASS: hybrid tea

HEIGHT: 3½–4 feet (105–120cm)

BLOOM SIZE: 4–4½ inches (10–11cm)

BLOOM TIME: repeats all summer

FRAGRANCE: slight

'Pascali'

An extraordinarily adaptable and beautiful white rose, 'Pascali' was voted The World's Favorite Rose at the 1991 World Federation of Rose Societies. Actually, it has quite a long and distinguished history of awards; among them a gold medal at The Hague in 1963, another gold medal at Portland in 1967, plus it was the All-America Selection winner in 1969. It is greatly valued for its ability to perform well in diverse climates, holding up to rain and hot sun with equal grace. The upright-growing, glossy-leaved plant is also winter-hardy, to Zone 5, at least.

But the flowers of 'Pascali' are what everyone raves about. Unlike some whites, these blooms are pure creamy white, untouched by pink or yellow hues. The petals are silky and substantial, and resist the rainspotting that mars other whites. The matter of fragrance has been debated—some claim it's sweet and delicious, others can detect no scent at all—so it is probably a matter of climate or other variable factors.

'Peace'

TYPE/CLASS: hybrid tea

HEIGHT: 5–6 feet (1.5–1.8m)

BLOOM SIZE: 6 inches (15cm)

BLOOM TIME: repeats all summer

FRAGRANCE: slight

'Peace'

The most cherished hybrid tea in the world created a sensation when it was introduced near the end of World War II. Its often-told story is certainly romantic: a rose-fancying U.S. embassy official smuggled budwood out of France just hours ahead of the invading German armies. The truth is less exciting, but still exhibits good timing. It was indeed developed in France, but the hybridizer, Francis Meilland, was able to ship it to various growers around the world before the war actually arrived on French soil. Its value was quickly recognized, and the rose was widely propagated. By 1945, it had become the floral symbol of the newly formed United Nations, and had taken top All-America Selections honors.

The appeal of the large double blossoms lies in the fact that no two are alike and that the color varies according to sunlight intensity. The dominant color is a beautiful warm yellow, but it is always enhanced with rose pink, usually along the edges of the petals and often flushing throughout, especially as the flower matures. You have to put your nose right in it to pick up the soft fragrance. Meanwhile, the large, dark green leaves are in scale, and have a leathery texture. 'Peace' looks good in nearly any setting, thanks to its robust form and adaptable color.

'Pink Meidiland'

TYPE/CLASS: shrub

HEIGHT: 4 feet (1.2m)

BLOOM SIZE: 2½ inches (6.5cm)

BLOOM TIME: repeats all summer

FRAGRANCE: none

'Pink Meidiland'

There's a whole series of Meidiland shrub roses, bred in France but becoming popular on both sides of the ocean. Bred to be low-maintenance, they are especially disease-resistant, require little pruning other than an annual spring trim, and are hardy in Zones 4 to 9. Generally speaking, you can count on them to bloom on and off all summer, and to produce attractive hips by autumn. The habit is dense and vigorous, ideal for mass plantings such as hedges, bank covers, or foundation plantings.

So far, these husky plants come in shades of white, red, fuchsia, and pink. And sometimes the flowers, which are borne in clusters, are double. 'Pink Meidiland' may be the most elegant of the lot, with sweet, single-petaled blooms of pink centered with a substantial creamy white eye and a neat boss of yellow stamens. It has been hailed as totally mildew-free, but it may get a little blackspot from time to time.

'Playboy'

TYPE/CLASS: floribunda

HEIGHT: 3 feet (90 cm)

BLOOM SIZE: 3½ inches (8cm)

BLOOM TIME: repeats all summer

FRAGRANCE: medium

'Playboy'

This is a compact plant with beautiful, vivacious blossoms. Cherry red petals are underlaid with glowing, coppery gold and centered with golden stamens. (The color holds for days on end, in the garden or in a bouquet.) Because the petal count is not high and the blooms are carried in great sprays, the overall effect is ruffly and fancy. And the scent is captivating—it's fresh and sweet, like ripe, crisp apples.

All this excitement is displayed on a dense, healthy-leaved bush that is lower growing than some floribundas. So even if you have a small garden, you can fit it in. A group planting would be sensational, or you can use 'Playboy' in a hot-colored border or as a container specimen.

'Pristine'

TYPE/CLASS: hybrid tea

HEIGHT: 4–7 feet (1.2–2m)

BLOOM SIZE: 5–6 inches (13–15cm)

BLOOM TIME: repeats all summer

FRAGRANCE: slight

'Pristine'

The name 'Pristine' certainly suits this pretty rose, which has an almost pearllike purity. The pink buds open to full-petaled blossoms that are ivory in the center, gradually yielding to a soft, sweet lavender-pink on the outer petals. As with many hybrid teas, the blossoms emerge from classic, urn-shaped buds, but these have a form so perfectly balanced that 'Pristine' has become a popular exhibition rose. They also have the unique and valuable quality of remaining poised in the attractive half-open stage for several days. As for fragrance, it seems to vary according to growing conditions and climate, but when present, is light and perfumey.

The foliage is also especially good. It's dark and glossy, rather large, and quite disease-resistant. Truly an elegant plant, 'Pristine' deserves a starring role and is well suited to formal-style gardens.

'Queen Elizabeth'

TYPE/CLASS: grandiflora

HEIGHT: 5–7 feet (1.5–2m)

BLOOM SIZE: 3–4 inches (7.5–10cm)

BLOOM TIME: repeats all summer

FRAGRANCE: medium

'Queen Elizabeth'

The tall, regal 'Queen Elizabeth' is in a class by itself—literally. She made her debut in 1955, and was to be the first of a glorious new class of taller, hardier roses—the grandifloras. But her triumph has never really been repeated (other so-called "grandifloras" lack her many distinctive virtues), and there are rose experts who scoff at the entire category. But nobody scoffs at her superb quality. Indeed, this rose has won more awards than perhaps any other, both in North America and abroad.

Like the best hybrid teas, 'Queen Elizabeth' has flawlessly formed blooms. They are a lovely medium to dark, watercolor-wash pink that in some climates is enriched with a touch of coral. Like the best floribundas, these are (usually) carried in great sprays. They have very long cutting stems, sometimes up to 3 feet (90cm) long!

'Queen Elizabeth' is also hardy and easy to grow. Tough and vigorous, it buoys the confidence of beginning gardeners and spares them the trouble of constant spraying. It shouldn't be pruned too much—it likes to be free to grow to its natural lofty heights. The best spot would be along a back fence or as a backdrop to a rose or mixed flower border.

'Rainbow's End'

TYPE/CLASS: miniature

HEIGHT: 10–14 inches (25–35cm)

BLOOM SIZE: 1½ inches (4cm)

BLOOM TIME: repeats all summer

FRAGRANCE: none

'Rainbow's End'

A lively, hot-colored flower, 'Rainbow's End' created a sensation when it was introduced by the great miniature rose breeder Harmon Saville in 1984. In 1986 it won an American Rose Society Award of Excellence; it has so many terrific qualities that it has continued to play a prominent role in miniature rose breeding ever since.

The blossoms are bright lemony yellow edged with scarlet (the amount of scarlet varies depending on exposure to sunlight). Each flower is a tiny replica of a hybrid tea bloom—high-centered and symmetrical. The plant is compact, healthy, and easy to grow. If you want bold, invigorating color and truly enchanting blooms but have limited space, 'Rainbow's End' could be the perfect solution. It can be overwintered in pots indoors.

'Rio Samba'

TYPE/CLASS: hybrid tea

HEIGHT: 5 feet (1.5m)

BLOOM SIZE: 5 inches (13cm)

BLOOM TIME: repeats all summer

FRAGRANCE: slight

'Rio Samba'

No doubt about it, there is something exotic about this rose, which won an All-America Rose Selections award in 1993. Each blossom is a spirited combination of hot yellow and fiery orange-scarlet. Unlike other color-blended roses, which gradually change from one color to another over a period of days, 'Rio Samba' displays its exciting mix from the moment the petals unfurl. Sturdy, long cutting stems will inspire you to cut bouquet after bouquet. Experiment with different color combinations; try building arrangements that include red roses or blazing yellow ones.

You might think that such a bright flower would be difficult to incorporate into the garden. And perhaps the most logical plan is to plant a group of three or more 'Rio Samba' bushes on their own. But the color really is more playful than strident, and you can certainly place a plant in the company of hot-colored perennials.

'Rise 'n' Shine'

TYPE/CLASS: miniature

HEIGHT: 14–18 inches (35–45cm)

BLOOM SIZE: 1½–1¾ inches (4–4.5cm)

BLOOM TIME: repeats all summer

FRAGRANCE: none

'Rise 'n' Shine'

This prolific plant is considered to be the best yellow miniature rose going. The plush little flowers are a sunny, pure yellow. They have no red or orange touches, nor do they fade out to a sickly pale near-white. And the show is non-stop, commencing in midsummer and continuing until cool weather arrives. It was given an American Rose Society Award of Excellence in 1978, and has not yet been topped.

The compact, rounded bush is liberally covered with medium green, disease-resistant leaves. Both the habit and the superior flowers mean you can rely on this plant to bring consistent, well-behaved color to your garden. 'Rise 'n' Shine' planted in quantity promises to bring a beam of cheer wherever you place it—whether it's along a walkway, lining a bed, or gracing a sunny corner.

Rosa banksiae var. *lutea*

(Yellow Lady Banks' rose)

TYPE/CLASS: climber (rambler)

HEIGHT: 20–30 feet (6–9m)

BLOOM SIZE: 1 inch (2.5cm)

BLOOM TIME: once in early summer

FRAGRANCE: slight

Rosa banksiae var. *lutea*

Sure, the yellow Lady Banks' rose has been described as a "house-eater," but if you want a big, billowing climber that's practically thorn-free, it will fit the bill perfectly. This glorious rose has been around for well over a century, and is commonly seen draping over old homes, arbors, porches, and even trees in the South. It also thrives in the West. Unfortunately, it is not hardy north of Zone 7.

The flowers appear in early summer, and while they don't repeat, they certainly earn their keep by lasting a long time, sometimes up to six weeks. They're petite, soft to deep yellow, laden with tiny petals, and carried in great sprays. The mild scent is reminiscent of violets. The foliage, meanwhile, is green and shiny, and the smooth canes have a naturally vertical habit that climbs eagerly. Anecdotal evidence suggests that deer don't like to nibble on this rose, so if you live in deer country, this feature is certainly an added attraction.

'Rosa Mundi'

(Rosa gallica var. versicolor)

TYPE/CLASS: shrub (gallica)

HEIGHT: 3–4 feet (90–120cm)

BLOOM SIZE: 3–3½ inches (7.5–8cm)

BLOOM TIME: blooms once in midsummer

FRAGRANCE: medium

'Rosa Mundi'

Once you see this intriguingly beautiful old-fashioned rose, you can never forget it. The semidouble blossoms, no two alike, sport cream to pale pink petals that are randomly striped, streaked with bright crimson, and centered by a bright spot of golden stamens. The effect is fresh and lively, and will make you think of a peppermint candy or a whimsical petticoat. The blossoms are also fragrant, wafting a sweet sachet scent into the air. In fact, both fragrance and color hold up well in potpourri.

For such a spunky, unusual flower, the plant is surprisingly tidy. However, like other gallicas, suckering may be a problem, and pruners should be kept close at hand just in case. The sage green foliage clothes the upright stems well. It is frequently used as a novel low hedge, which suits it.

Legend has it that it was named for "Fair Rosamund" Clifford, the mistress of Henry II of England. It's a charming thought but, alas, unlikely; the rose was first recorded around 1580, and Henry II lived from 1154 to 1189.

'Rose de Rescht'

TYPE/CLASS: shrub (damask)

HEIGHT: 2½–3½ feet (75–105cm)

BLOOM SIZE: 2–2½ inches (5–6.5cm)

BLOOM TIME: repeats all summer

FRAGRANCE: strong

'Rose de Rescht'

Sometimes wonderful things come in small packages. The blossoms of 'Rose de Rescht' aren't big and dramatic, but they are wonderfully lush and full (with up to one hundred petals!), almost like chrysanthemums. The color is vibrant, a rich, fuchsia-red with hints of royal purple. And the fragrance is completely ravishing. The blossoms begin appearing in early to midsummer and continue until autumn, when they are replaced by distinctive, tubular hips.

Even the plant is rather small, certainly for an antique shrub variety. It grows a little taller than wide, and is densely covered with medium green foliage. When young, the leaves are rimmed in red, making a pleasant counterpart to the early blooms. This rose is ideal if you have limited space and want old-fashioned looks and fragrance—with the bonus of repeat bloom.

'Rotes Meer'

TYPE/CLASS: rugosa hybrid

HEIGHT: 3 feet (90cm)

BLOOM SIZE: 3–4 inches (8–10cm)

BLOOM TIME: repeats all summer

FRAGRANCE: strong

'Rotes Meer'

There is no other crimson rose quite like this one. The color is amazingly pure, almost burgundy in its richness. Although the flowers are called double, the petals are arrayed in an elegant and neat cupped form. Golden stamens flash from the center. The long, unopened buds are a darker, wine red. Both flowers and buds are held well above the leaves so you can't miss them. And, like all rugosa roses, the flowers are clove-scented.

Another feature that sets this rugosa apart from the crowd is its compact size—most of its peers are big bushes.

Yet the leaves are not correspondingly small. They're still large, forest green, and crinkled (and durable, and highly disease-resistant). Imagine what a terrific low hedge it will make! You could certainly invite it into the heart of a perennial border, something you would never do with another rugosa.

Autumn color is also worth mentioning. The foliage of 'Rotes Meer' turns a soft gold and is accompanied by scarlet hips.

'Sea Pearl'

TYPE/CLASS: floribunda

HEIGHT: 3–5 feet (1–1.5m)

BLOOM SIZE: 4½ inches (11cm)

BLOOM TIME: repeats all summer

FRAGRANCE: medium

'Sea Pearl'

There's a lot of warmth in this long-blooming rose. The buds are pink and the first impression is pink, but its secret is that it does not stay a pure pink. Each petal on the bloom is gently underlaid with a soft glow of apricot-yellow. The fragrance is sweet, but you have to get up close to appreciate it. You'll also be pleased to discover long cutting stems.

The bush is tall for a floribunda, and has a sweeping, upright profile. Often the blooms are carried on the top of the plant (it blooms singly and in clusters). For these reasons, you can safely place this rose behind other ones or toward the rear of a flower border.

You can also count on this rose to be disease-resistant. The semiglossy leaves are dark green and lightly crinkled, and provide a handsome backdrop for the lovely blossoms.

'Sexy Rexy'

TYPE/CLASS: floribunda

HEIGHT: 3–5 feet (1–1.5m)

BLOOM SIZE: 3 inches (7.5cm)

BLOOM TIME: repeats all summer

FRAGRANCE: slight

'Sexy Rexy'

Admittedly, this rose is a bit of a novelty, and not just because of its name. The official explanation for the name is that it has proven to be a wonderful parent plant in hybridizing. Once you've grown it, you might also credit the incredibly generous, candelabralike flower clusters. Up to a hundred blooms per cluster prompted one nursery catalog to comment whimsically, "for which a vase has not yet been designed." Its 1984 introduction by renowned New Zealand breeder Sam McCredy inspired a flurry of

lively publicity in that country, including the bumper sticker "Have you Sexy Rexy in your rose bed?"

Be all that as it may, there's no denying it's a wonderful plant. The color is a splendid pastel pink, and the full-petaled form has an unexpected old-fashioned charm (many other modern floribundas have classic, hybrid tea–shaped blooms). The fact that it blooms readily all season long is also endearing, though you ought to deadhead for best results. The plant is on the tall side and has plenty of glossy green foliage.

'Simplicity'

TYPE/CLASS: shrub

HEIGHT: 4–5 feet (1.2–1.5m)

BLOOM SIZE: 3–4 inches (7.5–10cm)

BLOOM TIME: repeats all summer

FRAGRANCE: slight

'Simplicity'

Accurately named 'Simplicity', this is the original low-maintenance hedge rose, and probably still the best. Developed by the award-winning rose breeder Bill Warriner of Jackson & Perkins about fifteen years ago, it has proven immensely popular. And why not? It grows quickly and densely, is not fussy about soil, rarely requires spraying, and pumps out extraordinary numbers of blooms all summer long. The plants are also hardy, and because they're grown on their own roots rather than grafted, they're often able to repair winter damage with a spurt of new growth.

The medium pink flowers have a slightly cupped form and appear in clusters. It is also available in red, white, and only recently, yellow and purple. Flowers in the Simplicity series are handsome, if not particularly elegant, and generally offer a slight, pleasant fragrance.

The intended, and best, use of 'Simplicity' and its kin is as a "living fence." Plant in a long row at the base of a porch or along a property line, and savor the easy, dependable, colorful show.

'Sombreuil'

TYPE/CLASS: climber

HEIGHT: 8–15 feet (2.4–4.6m)

BLOOM SIZE: 3½–4 inches (8–10cm)

BLOOM TIME: repeats all summer

FRAGRANCE: medium

'Sombreuil'

A naturally graceful habit and long-blooming, old-fashioned flowers make an irresistible combination. The height varies according to where you grow it and how you prune it. 'Sombreuil' will take to a pillar as easily as a pergola. Its stems are pliable, though moderately thorny.

The exquisite blooms cover the entire length of the plant. The color is a heavy cream, sometimes blushed slightly with pink. There are loads of petals, but they're arranged (when the flower is fully open) in lush, symmetrical form. A rich, tea rose fragrance wafts into the air. And unlike some vintage roses, this one blooms repeatedly for the whole season.

Lovely 'Sombreuil' has only one major drawback. It's not very hardy, thriving mainly in warmer areas (Zones 7 and south). Northern gardeners who've lost their heart to her, however, can certainly try heroic winter-protection measures.

'Souvenir de la Malmaison'

TYPE/CLASS: shrub (Bourbon)

HEIGHT: 2–3 feet (60–90cm); 6–8 feet (1.8–2.4m) as a climber

BLOOM SIZE: 5 inches (13cm)

BLOOM TIME: once in midsummer

FRAGRANCE: strong

'Souvenir de la Malmaison'

Named after Empress Josephine's renowned rose garden on the outskirts of Paris, 'Souvenir de la Malmaison' is utterly magnificent when grown under optimum conditions. It requires warm, sunny, dry weather to thrive and bloom to its full potential. Rain completely dampens its spirits!

Note that this rose comes in two forms. Both bush and climber are comparatively short, and either one would be a suitable choice for a tight space or a smaller garden.

However, like other Bourbons, the blossoms are big and full. A soft, baby pink at every stage, they're deliciously scented. They start out cupped but eventually splay out to a flat form that reveals the generous load of petals. The plant tends to bloom later than most roses, and not very lushly. But it is so beautiful, you quickly forgive the limited performance.

'Starina'

TYPE/CLASS: miniature

HEIGHT: 12 inches (30cm)

BLOOM SIZE: 1½ inches (4cm)

BLOOM TIME: repeats all summer

FRAGRANCE: none

'Starina'

Although it made its debut more than thirty years ago, 'Starina' remains a star in the miniature rose world to this day, and is widely available. It is credited with being the first miniature to have blossoms that truly mimicked the elegant form of classic hybrid tea roses, a form it displays with perfect grace from bud to fully open bloom.

The semiglossy, dark green foliage makes a handsome stage for the warm and inviting orange-red blooms. With an agreeable, slightly spreading habit, the plant is as wide as it is tall. One plant in a pot on a patio or deck will be much admired. But a miniature of this quality could also line a path to a door or garden gate in great style.

'Sunsprite'

'Sunsprite'

TYPE/CLASS: floribunda

HEIGHT: 3 feet (90cm)

BLOOM SIZE: 3 inches (7.5cm)

BLOOM TIME: repeats all summer

FRAGRANCE: strong

This terrific bloomer may very well be the best yellow floribunda. It has everything going for it: high-quality blooms, fragrance, and toughness. As is typical of floribundas, the smallish flowers are carried in clusters that display them at various stages of opening. The buds of 'Sunsprite' are a rich, buttery yellow before they unfurl to a sunny, chiffon yellow. The scent, apparent even before you get right up next to the bush, is fresh and spicy, like a sweet cinnamon coffeecake.

But what may really sell you on the plant is its durability. When other yellows flag, or fade to white in the hot summer sun, 'Sunsprite' remains sprightly. And unlike many other yellows, the bright green foliage is mildew-resistant. Last but not least, the plant is winter-hardy, and can easily be grown up to Zone 6 (north of there, be sure to shield it). Plant this one wherever your garden needs really dependable, bright color.

'Sutter's Gold'

TYPE/CLASS: hybrid tea

HEIGHT: 4–4½ feet (1.2–1.3m)

BLOOM SIZE: 4–5 inches (10–13cm)

BLOOM TIME: repeats all summer

FRAGRANCE: strong

'Sutter's Gold'

Neither pure yellow nor pure orange, but a glowing golden color somewhere in between, this magnificent rose has a haunting, summer-evening feel to it. It's an eager and prolific bloomer, starting early in the season (sometimes it's the very first rose to get going) and continuing on and off until autumn. The buds are classically shaped, but the open flower's form is looser and less formal than some hybrid teas. The fragrance is especially strong and fruity.

The bush is also super. It's an average height for hybrid teas, but it grows a little narrower than most, so you can squeeze it into a more confined spot if need be. This rose would be a good addition to a spring-flowering shrub border, bringing welcome color after those blooms have faded. Try it adjacent to anything with russet- or bronze-tinged leaves. Mercifully, thorns are rather light on 'Sutter's Gold'.

'Sweet Chariot'

TYPE/CLASS: miniature

HEIGHT: 18–24 inches (45–60cm)

BLOOM SIZE: 1½ inches (4cm)

BLOOM TIME: repeats all summer

FRAGRANCE: strong

'Sweet Chariot'

It's not often that you see a miniature in this color. 'Sweet Chariot' is not mauve or lavender, but rather a dark crimson-purple. The flowers are laden with many petals and carried in exuberant sprays. And the fragrance—unusually strong for a miniature—is rich and heady. Imagine what sweet little bouquets you can harvest!

The matte green leaves provide a nice contrast to the blooms. Although these bushy plants spread to the sides a bit more than some of their peers, you can still grow 'Sweet Chariot' in a container. Just make sure it has enough elbow room. In the garden proper, you will find it to be a steadfast performer and super-hardy. If you combine it with other flowers, choose bold companions such as a bright yellow miniature. 'Sweet Chariot' and 'Rise 'n' Shine' make a stunning combination.

'Therese Bugnet'

TYPE/CLASS: rugosa hybrid

HEIGHT: 4–6 feet (1.2–1.8m)

BLOOM SIZE: 4 inches (10cm)

BLOOM TIME: repeats all summer

FRAGRANCE: strong

'Therese Bugnet'

If a trouble-free, super-hardy, fragrant pink rose sounds like heaven to you, look no further. Bred in Canada and descended from the extraordinarily tough, disease-resistant rugosa roses, 'Therese Bugnet' is a real winner. It is hardy to Zone 2, which covers all of the United States and a good portion of Canada, so just about anyone can grow it.

It is also very pretty. The buds begin in a rich lilac to red, and burst open to big, ruffly saucers of mauve-tinged pink. A cluster that contains both stages makes a darling bouquet. You'll also savor the rich cinnamon-clove fragrance.

The plant is taller than some of its relatives, and often used as a hedge. The distinctive leaves are narrow and dark blue-green. Also, the plant's thorns, while certainly present, are not as plentiful as you might expect (new shoots are practically thornless).

'Touch of Class'

TYPE/CLASS: hybrid tea

HEIGHT: 5–6 feet (1.5–1.8m)

BLOOM SIZE: 4½–5½ inches

BLOOM TIME: repeats all summer

FRAGRANCE: none

'Touch of Class'

Hobbyists and professionals who exhibit roses competitively rave about 'Touch of Class'. And those of us who may never take our love of roses that far should certainly pay attention. Its color is obviously a factor: the blossoms are gorgeous, beginning as a warm coral and mellowing to a rich, salmon-pink, underlaid with a barely perceptible cream reverse. The form, too, is outstanding, with long, shapely buds that spiral open to high-centered blossoms with slightly ruffled petals. The petals are heavy-textured, which makes for a long life on the plant or in bouquets. As for the stems, they are a bouquet-maker's dream—long, strong, and straight.

The plant itself is less perfect. The dark green foliage looks durable, but is vulnerable to mildew and must be sprayed regularly if this disease is a problem in your area. Also, 'Touch of Class' can grow rather tall for a hybrid tea, so you'll want to place it where it won't block out other plants.

'Tropicana'

TYPE/CLASS: hybrid tea

HEIGHT: 4–5 feet (1.2–1.8m)

BLOOM SIZE: 5–6 inches (13–15cm)

BLOOM TIME: repeats all summer

FRAGRANCE: strong

'Tropicana'

It's possible that this knockout hybrid tea has suffered from too much adulation. In the thirty-five-plus years since it was introduced, it has won many coveted awards. Naturally, it is widely available, but you may notice that it is conspicuously absent from some rose catalogs and reference books, as if the pros have grown weary of its great popularity.

Nonetheless, it remains a great rose. The color is a fiery, almost fluorescent blend of orange, coral, and crimson. And the massive bloom size demands attention even from many yards away. The Jackson & Perkins catalog describes the fragrance as a "rich, fruit-filled perfume with notes of ripe raspberries and exotic citrus." Anyone who has smelled 'Tropicana' will not dismiss this as catalog hyperbole. The plant is tall and robust and boasts long cutting stems. Foliage is dark and substantial; but gardeners in humid areas find it gets mildew.

But where, oh where, are you going to place a rose like this? You might want keep it out of the traditional rose bed (where it will overwhelm almost any other color). Try it instead in the company of foliage plants, such as purple barberries or silvery artemisias, and savor the glory.

'Tuscany Superb'

TYPE/CLASS: shrub (gallica)

HEIGHT: 3–4 feet (90–120cm)

BLOOM SIZE: 3½–4 inches (8–10cm)

BLOOM TIME: once in early to midsummer

FRAGRANCE: strong

'Tuscany Superb'

Why grow a rose that only blooms once a year? A rose as beautiful and richly fragrant as 'Tuscany Superb' will certainly tempt you. The lush-petaled blossoms are truly glorious: deep crimson brushed with black, and a seductive, velvety texture to match. They're centered by a royal flash of golden stamens. The heady, almost winelike fragrance will make you swoon. (Like other gallica roses, the petals of this one hold their color and scent well in potpourris and sachets.)

This vigorous plant grows perhaps a little taller than wide, and is fairly bushy. The leaves are dark forest green, and resist pests and diseases, with the exception of occasional bouts with blackspot. The stems aren't very thorny, although you may encounter some small bristles.

One last word in favor of its blooming habit: it means you can plant 'Tuscany Superb' in a spot where later-blooming perennials that might clash with the distinctive color won't yet have made their appearance.

'William Baffin'

TYPE/CLASS: climber (kordesii)

HEIGHT: 7–10 feet (2–3m)

BLOOM SIZE: 2½ inches (6.5cm)

BLOOM TIME: repeats all summer

FRAGRANCE: none

'William Baffin'

Far northern gardeners take note: this may be the only repeat-blooming climber currently available to you. Super-hardiness (proven to Zone 3, and claimed for Zone 2 by its Canadian breeders) is not its only virtue, however.

'William Baffin' is a truly pretty rose. The plant begins blooming in early summer, when it literally cascades with bright pink flowers centered with sunny yellow stamens. In warmer areas, the petals sometimes develop a splash of white markings near the middle. The clusters may contain as many as thirty blooms apiece! The show continues steadily throughout the summer months and slows down only when autumn arrives. As an added benefit, the foliage is exceptionally disease-resistant. In fact, 'William Baffin' has never been known to have blackspot and mildew is rare.

To get the best performance out of this superior rose, grow it in full sun. There, you can count on it to be vigor-ous and gorgeous. Note that it may not reach its full height in colder zones, where a fence or pillar would be its best climbing surface. Otherwise, feel free to train it over any arch or trellis.

'Winsome'

TYPE/CLASS: miniature

HEIGHT: 18–24 inches (45–60cm)

BLOOM SIZE: 1½ inches (4cm)

BLOOM TIME: repeats all summer

FRAGRANCE: none

'Winsome'

A rather large and exceptionally prolific miniature, 'Winsome' sports jaunty, bright lavender to mauve (sometimes almost red) blooms of high quality. They're double, but elegantly formed in hybrid tea style. And the petals are heavy textured, which allows them to last a long time on the bush or in a flower arrangement.

The plant is quite bushy and grows taller than most of its peers, so you'll want to grow it in the ground. Its good health and sweetheart blooms would be a welcome addition to a moderate-height perennial border. 'Winsome' won an Award of Excellence from the American Rose Society in 1985.

'Zéphirine Drouhin'

TYPE/CLASS: climber (Bourbon)

HEIGHT: 8–12 feet (2.4–3.7m)

BLOOM SIZE: 3 ½–4 inches (8–10cm)

BLOOM TIME: repeats all summer

FRAGRANCE: strong

'Zéphirine Drouhin'

Introduced way back in 1868 and beloved to this day, 'Zéphirine Drouhin' is a fetchingly beautiful repeat-bloomer. Buds are long and dark pink and open to flowers in a rich, deep shade of pink. The powerful, romantic scent has a touch of raspberry to it. New growth is coppery purple, which provides a stunning contrast, but it eventually becomes a handsome and disease-resistant dark green. Even the thornless stems contribute to the show—they're burgundy.

As if she needed more selling points, 'Zéphirine Drouhin' is also shade-tolerant and handles alkaline soil and pollution better than most roses, which will entice city gardeners. Because of its medium height, this rose is ideal for training on a post or pillar. And its lack of thorns makes it a natural choice for training up and over a frequently trafficked archway or porch. Hardiness seems to be the sole concern, as the plant is rated only to Zone 6. With protection, however, it could be grown farther north.

PLANT HARDINESS ZONES

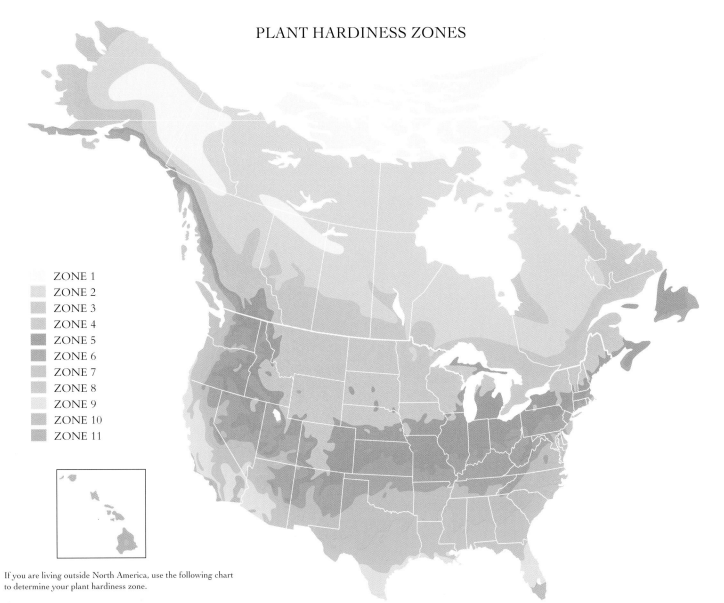

ZONE 1
ZONE 2
ZONE 3
ZONE 4
ZONE 5
ZONE 6
ZONE 7
ZONE 8
ZONE 9
ZONE 10
ZONE 11

If you are living outside North America, use the following chart to determine your plant hardiness zone.

Range of Average Annual Minimum Temperatures for Each Zone

	Fahrenheit (°F)	Celsius (°C)
Zone 1	Below –50°	Below –45.6°
Zone 2	–50° to –40°	–45.6° to –40°
Zone 3	–40° to –30°	–40° to –34.4°
Zone 4	–30° to –20°	–34.4° to –28.9°
Zone 5	–20° to –10°	–28.9° to –23.3°
Zone 6	–10° to 0°	–23.3° to –17.8°
Zone 7	0° to 10°	–17.8° to –12.2°
Zone 8	10° to 20°	–12.2° to –6.7°
Zone 9	20° to 30°	–6.7° to –1.1°
Zone 10	30° to 40°	–1.1° to 4.4°
Zone 11	Above 40°	Above 4.4°

Sources

Here you'll find some good mail-order rose nurseries (retail) in the U.S. and Canada:

Antique Rose Emporium
Rte. 5, Box 143
Brenham, TX 77833
Catalog $5

Blossoms & Bloomers
E. 11415 Krueger La.
Spokane, WA 99207
Catalog $1

Carroll Gardens
444 E. Main St.
Westminster, MD 21157
Catalog $3

Edmunds' Roses
6235 S.W. Kahle Rd.
Wilsonville, OR 97070
Free catalog

Hardy Roses for the North
Box 273
Danville, WA 99121-0273
Catalog $3

Heirloom Old Garden Roses
24062 N.E. Riverside Dr.
St. Paul, OR 97137
Catalog $5

Jackson & Perkins Co.
One Rose La.
Medford, OR 97501
Free catalog

Justice Miniature Roses
5947 S.W. Kahle Rd.
Wilsonville, OR 97070
Free catalog

Lowe's Own-Root Roses
6 Sheffield Rd.
Nashua, NH 03062
Catalog $2

Nor'East Miniature Roses
P.O. Box 307
Rowley, MA 01969
Free catalog

The Roseraie at Bayfields
P.O. Box R
Waldoboro, ME 04572
Catalog free for first-class stamp

Royall River Roses
70 New Gloucester Rd.
North Yarmouth, ME 04097
Catalog $3

Wayside Gardens
1 Garden La.
Hodges, SC 29695
Free catalog

White Flower Farm
Rte. 63
Litchfield, CT 06759
Free catalog

Canadian Sources

Hortico, Inc.
723 Robson Rd., R.R. #1
Waterdown, Ontario L0R 2H1
Canada
Catalog $3

V. Kraus Nurseries Ltd.
P.O. Box 180
Carlisle, Ontario L0R 1H0
Canada
Catalog $1

Pickering Nurseries, Inc.
670 Kingston Rd.
Pickering, Ontario L1V 1A6
Canada
Catalog $3

Following are rose societies that offer information on growing roses:

American Rose Society
P.O. Box 30,000
Shreveport, LA 71130-0030
(318) 938-5402

Canadian Rose Society
10 Fairfax Crescent
Scarborough, Ontario M1L 1Z8
Canada
(416) 757-8809

Other Useful Addresses:

The Combined Rose List
Peter Schneider
P.O. Box 677
Montua, OH 44255

Import Permit:
Permit Unit
USDA, PPQ
Federal Building
Room 638
Hyattsville, MD 20782